Decks & Patios

Inspiration & Information for the Do-It-Yourselfer

Martin Miller

CREATIVE
PUBLISHING
international

CHANHASSEN, MINNESOTA

www.creativepub.com

CREATIVE
PUBLISHING
international

Copyright © 2005
Creative Publishing International, Inc.
18705 Lake Drive East
Chanhassen, Minnesota 55317
1-800-328-3895
www.creativepub.com
All rights reserved

Printed in China
10 9 8 7 6 5 4 3 2 1

President/CEO: Ken Fund
Vice President/Publisher: Linda Ball
*Vice President/Retail Sales
  & Marketing:* Kevin Haas

Executive Editor: Bryan Trandem
Creative Director: Tim Himsel
Managing Editor: Michelle Skudlarek
Editorial Director: Jerri Farris

The Lexicon Group
108 3rd Street, Suite 212
Des Moines, IA 50309
515-243-4615
Executive Director: Catherine M. Staub, Ed.D.
President: James A. Stepp
Writer: Martin Miller
Designer: Bill Nelson
Cover Design: Lexicon Consulting, Inc.
Photography: Lexicon Consulting, Inc.
Editorial Assistant: Julie M. Collins
Photo Researcher: Jessi Siddell

IdeaWise: Decks & Patios

Library of Congress
Cataloging-in-Publication Data

Miller, Martin, 1944-
  Ideawise decks & patios :
inspiration & information for the
do-it-yourselfer / by Martin Miller.
       p. cm.
  Includes index.
  ISBN 1-58923-178-3 (soft cover)
  1. Decks (Architecture, Domestic) 2.
Porches. I. Title.
  690' .893--dc22   2004024881

Table of Contents

Shades of grey help tuck this patio spot right into its rocky landscape. The greys create a hushed tone that's perfect for a quiet gathering, and the colorful plantings add just the right amount of visual contrast.

Introduction

When decks and patios first appeared on the backs of post-war homes, they not only became an instant success, they became part of the American dream. And it's no wonder. Something about the outdoors tugs at all of us.

Whether we just need to retreat into the open air after being closed in our workplaces or simply need the fundamental replenishment that only nature can provide, our love of the outdoors runs deep. How else can we explain that these early structures—modest, undecorated, and for the most part, unattractive—could have grown into the often elaborate outdoor rooms they are today?

It's true that the American lifestyle was moving off the front porch, with its open-air view to the public and passers-by and into the back yard, where family and friends could gather in a more private setting. But our attachment to decks and patios runs deeper than a mere change in family lifestyle. Perhaps it is best explained by a contradiction—at the same time we're trying to get away from it all, we don't want to leave home to do it. We'd rather nest, cocoon. That's what a deck or patio does for us. It gives us a way to enjoy the outdoors without ever having to leave home. It's such a strong attachment that each year, over a million American homeowners add a deck or patio to their house. So if you're dreaming of your own deck or patio, whether you live on a small city lot or sprawling country estate, you've got plenty of company.

*T*urning your back yard into a safe haven for morning breakfast, quiet reading, family activities, or just plain stargazing can mean building a solitary respite or constructing a large, multi-purpose outdoor room. No matter what your goals are and no matter how much you just can't wait to enjoy the laid-back atmosphere of your outdoor space, the time for laying back is later. Inventing the atmosphere requires some creative planning.

In many respects, designing an outdoor space resembles designing an interior room, only with a lot more freedom. First, you're going at it from the ground up. Outdoor dimensions are larger, there's no existing color palette to contend with, no doorway where you want to put a piece of important furniture. Because they open up to the sky and the sun, decks and patios offer almost unlimited freedom of expression—and that can be a problem.

If you find yourself a bit overwhelmed by the very abundance of choices, you might want to enlist the aid of a landscape architect or landscape designer. Get an architect for the big stuff—changing the terrain or making a major alteration to the architecture of your home. A designer can help you find just the right style—your style. You'll likely find it an investment, not an expense. Besides, what often happens is that you find out your ideas were a whole lot better in the first place than you imagined. You can even go on-line to find Internet sites complete with free interactive design tools. More sophisticated software is available for a fee and gives you hours of electronic experimentation.

Look for ways to build in benches, especially on long stretches of low-lying platform decks. Built-ins help define the perimeter of a deck and keep seating out of the middle of the space

The definition of patio is not confined by size. Circular brickwork gives this small spot its own special identity, asking you to stop and sit a spell. The herringbone pattern seems to have no beginning or end within the circle. We may not consciously perceive the effect of these subtle geometries, but they make their mark nevertheless.

Use the lines and colors of your house as cues to help you integrate your outdoor space with its surroundings.

One of the first choices you'll probably encounter is "Deck? Or patio?" But don't answer that question right away. That perfect spot for your patio might turn out to be too steep— better suited to the tall posts of a deck vaulting over it. Perhaps that deck of your dreams really would look better in the terraced landscape as a series of cascading patios, each connected with crushed-stone paths.

Sometimes it might be materials that change your mind. You've had your heart set on a flagstone patio because you like the dignified sense of permanence it will bring to your yard. Then you encounter Ipe, a South American hardwood, and you realize you can create that same atmosphere with a rich color and without the maintenance that other woods can require. Or your vision of your backyard has had "deck" written all over it until you see one of the infinite geometric designs possible with precast pavers—at a fraction of the cost and without any future maintenance fuss.

You might even go so far as to build both a deck and a patio. There's almost no combination of materials that won't work well together. Wood and stone or other hardscape materials make pleasing contrasts, and will give you an excellent way of defining space—reserving the spot for family dining and distinguishing it from party space, for example.

Your planning choices will obviously be affected by terrain and materials. Local building codes may also have something to say about your outdoor space—where you put it, what materials you use, and how you construct it. Before you get too far down the road, stop off at your building department and show them what you have in mind. Building officials have a wealth of information that can help you make good choices.

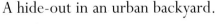

A hide-out in an urban backyard.
"Urban landscape" doesn't have to be an oxymoron. Small though they are, big-city lots offer an abundance of design opportunities. The limitation of their size can be their chief asset, providing city dwellers with built-in spots for getting away from the hustle of their environment. Details count in small spaces—the effect of color, texture, line, and pattern are magnified and call for careful planning.

How to Use This Book

The pages of *IdeaWise Decks & Patios* are packed with images of interesting, attractive, efficient decks and patios. And although we hope you enjoy looking at them, they're more than pretty pictures: they're inspiration accompanied by descriptions, facts, and details meant to help you plan your deck or patio project wisely.

Some of the decks and patios you see here will suit your sense of style, while others may not appeal to you at all. If you're serious about renovating or rejuvenating your landscape, read every page—there's as much to learn in what you don't like as in what you do. Look at each photograph carefully and take notes. The details you gather are the seeds from which ideas for your new project will sprout.

IdeaWise Decks & Patios contains seven chapters: Destinations, Style, Decking, Pattern & Rhythm, Materials, Comfort, Amenities, and Furnishings. In each chapter, you'll find several features, each of which contains a specific type of wisdom.

*Design***Wise** features hints and tips—insider tricks—from professional landscape designers. Special thanks to Jolly Roberts; Timothy Jones, Jones Brothers Construction; James P. Teske, Centerville Landscaping; Christopher Mikol, American Beauty Landscaping, Inc.; Greg Smith of Adolph S. Rosekrans, Inc., Architects; and Chaden Halfhill, Silent Rivers Design-Build.

*Dollar***Wise** describes money-saving ideas that can be adapted to your own plans and circumstances.

*Idea***Wise** illustrates a clever do-it-yourself project for each topic.

We've also included *Words to the Wise,* when we thought it would help to define some terms which might be unfamiliar.

Another important feature of *IdeaWise Decks & Patios* is the Resource Guide on page 136. The Resource Guide contains as much information as possible about the decks and patios in this book, including contact information for designers and manufacturers, when available.

DesignWise

Jolly Roberts
Landscape Architect
Auburn, Alabama

• When planning a deck or patio, list the activities you want to enjoy. What furnishings will you need? For how many?

• What size? Spaces can seem smaller out doors than in. Draw furniture to scale on your plan. Leave ample room for moving around seating and tables.

• Sketch your yard on graph paper, noting good views, sun and shade, privacy, slopes, and drainage. Slopes will require decks, or grading and possibly retaining walls, to create a level space.

• The general rule is—keep outdoor activities near related rooms—dining and grilling near the kitchen, entertaining near the living room. Break the rule to enjoy great views, water, or other site features.

• A few dimensions:
Dining for two—8' to 10' diameter; for four—12' diameter.
Standing room—5 sq. ft. per person.
Main passageway—4' wide.
Wall seating—24" high maximum and a minimum of 2 linear feet per person.

DollarWise

You want a redwood deck, but your budget says no. Use less expensive lumber where it won't show—for posts, beams, and joists. You could save enough to use the better looking woods for the railing and decking. Stamped concrete or precast pavers will give you a "brick" or "flagstone" patio at a fraction of the cost.

IdeaWise

Paint yourself a charming pattern. If the additional cost of framing required puts a fancy decking pattern beyond your reach, try painting a pattern. Use high quality alkyd deck paints and alternate their colors and shapes using stencils. The paint will wear off, of course, but the wood texture and color showing through will only add to the charm of your design. This idea works best when you want to create the look of a quaint cottage and with gray untreated woods.

Words to the Wise

You may hear the terms "dry set" and "mortared" (or "wet set") when you're out shopping for paving. What's the difference?

• **Dry-set** (or "sand-set") paving is brick, flagstone, or precast pavers that are set in a sand base. That sound easy enough, but there's more to it. Dry-set installations require a 6- to 8-inch gravel sub base for drainage. Landscape fabric usually goes over that (to keep the sand from migrating down through the rock), then a 2-inch sand bed. The paving is laid on this bed, and the joints are swept full with fine sand.

• **Mortared** paving is any material adhered to a concrete slab with cement-based or thinset mortar. This installation also requires a gravel subbase, then a 3 to 4 inch level concrete slab, a 2-inch mortar bed, then the paving itself. Joints are typically wider than in a sand-set site and are filled with mortar or grout.

Which is better?

Mortared patios are less likely to heave during winter. Dry-set surfaces are generally easier to install and repair. Pre-cast pavers should be sand-set only. Ceramic tile always means mortaring the material.

CHAPTER 1

Destinations

Suppose for a moment that you don't yet have a deck or patio—which, if you're reading these words, is likely. Suppose, too, that you want one and don't know where to begin. It's actually easier than you think. Because for all that decks and patios offer (and they offer plenty), the most important opportunity they offer is a chance for a quick getaway, an opportunity to take a small vacation. Right in your own backyard. So to begin, imagine your deck or patio as a destination, a vacation spot, not just a flat place somewhere out there in the yard. And, what's the first thing you do when you plan a vacation? You probably make a list of all the things you want to do when you get there. Planning a deck or patio is quite similar.

Decks and patios enhance your lifestyle, expand your living space, ease the transition between your house and yard, bring the indoors out, and make your landscape more attractive. They do all that, and then they'll return your investment if you sell your home. But those are just the facts. What's really behind the wish for a deck or patio is that you want out—outdoors, that is. And you want an outdoor haven that's close to the comforts of home.

So, whether you want to entertain, share meals with family, gather small groups of friends together, lounge around in the spa or pool, hang out while the kids play, or just sit and take in nature's picture show, here's what you do. Make a list of everything everyone in the family wants to do in their new "vacation" spot. You might have to pare it back some because your landscape or your budget won't let you do all the things you want. But everything for your deck or patio—the shape of the space, where you put it, what it's going to look like, and whether it will have running water and electricity—comes from that list.

Still feeling a little disconcerted? Turn the page. We'll show you how.

Respites & Retreats

A spot for coffee and the morning paper before the clamor of the day begins. Space just large enough for you and your favorite unfinished book. A place for sitting or just catching a breath. All of us need quiet space from time to time. Respites and retreats don't demand much. At a minimum they require only a simple bench or single chair, something behind you (or overhead), and maybe a few of your favorite things. Look for an unused corner of the yard, a shady place along the backyard fence; steal a piece of solitude from the garden.

Simplicity is the key to comfort and good design. Achieving it requires that you know what to leave out. Dappled shade, straight lines, simple shapes, and a couple of contrasting colors all work together in this deck-corner haven.

The hip-roofed pergola and angled rafters enhance the quiet identity of this secluded space. They also provide both guaranteed and filtered shade. Aged redwood helps blend this structure into its natural surroundings.

The "footprint" of this retreat occupies just the right amount of space for quiet contemplation and doesn't overpower the landscape.

Decks and patios don't have to be attached to the house. They

don't have to be attached to anything. A detached structure lets you create a quiet space of your own design, unhindered by the walls and angles of your home.

Tall shrubs shelter the space from outside views and harsh winds.

The redwood arbor, partially hidden, invites you to view the garden.

Plants in pots add a colorful contrast against the neutral background of graying timbers and green foliage.

You don't need much to create a **quiet spot,** even on a busy deck. What's most important is that the space have its own identity, with attributes that clearly distinguish the space as made for private use. Even a few potted plants and carefully placed accents are often enough to do the trick.

This clever planter not only adds visual interest, it implies that there's a "ceiling" above this otherwise open private spot.

The blue clay pot and birdbath "planter stand" contrast sharply with the shingles and decking, helping to clearly identify this space as reserved for contemplation.

Lightweight chairs and table can be moved around the deck to follow the shade.

The wooden bench tucked into the trees makes this a respite that's always ready and waiting.

Container-grown plants brighten the spot when the landscape doesn't provide room for garden beds.

Flagstone set in soil provides a contrasting —and dry— transition between the lawn and decking.

Working with nature, not against it. The edge of this site ends abruptly at a steep dropoff into the woods, and the railing winds along the edge of the terrain. Here, a rectangular surface would have seemed less at home than the natural contours of this small deck.

Just for sitting. You don't need much room for a solitary retreat. Just a chair and a few flagstones or modular decking sections set in sand right in the soil will do nicely. You'll feel more secure if you place the back of the chair to a wall or fence and give yourself an open view or garden to look out to.

Dinner for Two (or more)

What could be more romantic, or more festive, or more relaxing than outdoor dining? No matter what the occasion, a deck or patio offers flexibility and enhances the experience of sharing a meal. To start with, food seems to taste better outdoors. Add an ambience that fits the occasion and you'll have *al fresco* dining that even the most elaborate interior room can't equal. Whether you're planning a table for two or a full-out neighborhood barbecue, let your lifestyle dictate your design. Intimate occasions won't need more than a few square feet of space. Large gatherings call for ample table tops and seating. At a minimum, you can fit a grill and a small table and chairs into a 250-square-foot outdoor room, with space for easy access. If you're short on space but long on parties, design elements of your deck or patio so they do double duty. A wide cap rail doubles as a "table" for beverages and plates. Deep steps become comfortable seating. Stored folding chairs can rescue a host facing an overflow crowd. No two designs will ever be the same. Whether you plan to wheel out the grill, cook on a stainless outdoor kitchen, or cater yourself from the kitchen, design your outdoor room to meet your needs.

Dramatic contrasts create unique designs. Who would have thought that a sheer white cloth draped loosely over a side table next to a rocky stream could create such intimacy? Yet the stark formality and the rough textures work perfectly together to make this a one-of a-kind setting.

Repeated tints of the same hue— red-brown wood tones and the reds in the railing and table cover—help unify this raised-deck dining space.

Built-in benches offer a practical solution to seating in narrow spaces. They take up less room than commercial furnishings.

The narrow table is sized to fit the confines of the deck. You may have to special-order undersized furnishings for small spaces, but the slight additional cost more than pays for itself in added convenience.

Color is the most volatile of design elements. Too much of it can overpower a scene. Too little leaves the space bland and uninviting. Using different shades of the same color can unify a space without dominating it. Look for ways to give the colors of your dinner setting a backdrop, like the green trees of the landscape and the wood tones of the decking.

Giving a vine a trellis to grow on not only brings color to a space, it provides an inexpensive way to add an artistic accent.

Convenient access to the kitchen is extremely important for outdoor dining space without room for a grill or built-in cooking facilities.

Although the redwood deck and shingles unify the area, too much of the same thing can be numbing. Unity will always benefit from variety and contrast, provided here by the green trim and foliage.

The back rail helps define the area and leaves plenty of room for serving. The gap between the rails makes the design seem less confining.

Circles create intimacy. Here, the angles of the bench and rail create a "horseshoe" that brings the family together at the meal.

Shelter, shade, and seclusion all combine seamlessly in this cozy family dining space. Look for inside corners of your house in which to nest your deck or patio. The walls provide built-in privacy.

Breakfast or brunch, the elements of this outdoor dinette are always inviting. Set on a traditional mortared flagstone floor, the curved white benches add a contrasting elegance to the almost rural setting. Modern furniture finishes such as polyester powders are impervious to almost every kind of weather and wear.

Nature's built-in informality does not rule out formal dining. In fact, formal out-door design schemes are as welcoming and comfortable as any casual cottage-garden setting.

Evergreen shrubs provide needed privacy.

Muted brown furnishings complement the tones of the untreated redwood deck, but offer a stylistic contrast.

Low built-in bench offers additional seating or a place for casual conversation while dinner is being prepared.

Railings ensure safety and help separate the dining area from the remaining land-scape.

Black-iron trellis breaks up the expanse of the blue wall, provides an eye-catching accent and perhaps an espalier on which to train a flowering vine.

Sometimes it helps to paint yourself into a corner, especially when you're trying to make a room of your own along the back wall of a row-house complex. The blue wall also conveniently hides an air conditioning unit on the adjacent property.

A well-planned deck or patio extends a standing invitation. That means its colors, lines, textures, and materials should all conspire to keep you there. Here, the red director's chairs, the muted tones of mortared flagstone and the support posts, and the landscaping beyond the covered patio do just that.

Gatherings

A well-designed deck or patio that invites you outdoors is, by its very nature, made for gatherings. Ask yourself questions that will help you plan the size and shape of your outdoor room. Do you want (or only have room for) small-group get-togethers? Are lavish parties in your blood? Or both? The right space can do more than one job. Try things out before finalizing your plan. Mark the area of your proposed deck or patio site with paint. Then bring in the lounges, tables and chairs, the grill, and containers for flowers. Use interior furniture in a pinch and add about two square feet more per chair. Make sure you have enough comfortable room before you draw your plans.

Make use of natural shade whenever possible.

Outdoor living always carries something of the unpredictable and generates more excitement than indoor activities. Here the white chairs add drama to the setting under the massive dark trunk of an old oak.

Incorporate trees and other natural elements (like streams and large rocks) into your design. But make sure trees and shrubs have room to grow (and bend in a strong wind if they're as large as this one).

Transform an unadorned edge with built-in seating or planting boxes.

Wicker works wonders in almost any setting. It's the perfect product for any style. You can paint it to match your outdoor space or its surroundings, and its very look and lines say "comfortable."

*Idea*Wise

If your deck or patio seems cramped, maybe it's not the space at all. Maybe it's the furniture. Or rather, where you've put it. Try a rearrangement. Keep furnishings, especially over-stuffed items like lounge chairs, out of the center of your deck or patio so traffic can flow freely through the central space. If there's only one "center" on your deck or patio, keeping it open will help make it feel more spacious.

All untreated woods turn grey in time. Some hold up better than others. If it's the natural look you're after, choose the species that will give you the longest life for the money.

Because of their height, raised decks often don't need as much privacy. Use an open baluster design to let the view come through (but check local codes for safety spacing). Plexiglass panels work well here, too.

Look for views when planning. Build your deck or patio to take advantage of them. If you have a vista you can't live without, but it's hidden from first-floor view, what about a second-story deck? Raised decks often open to the sky. Take a look through your upper windows. You might see things you've missed before. Put the space below to good use—for family meals, entertaining, or storage.

The open squares that outline the pergola pillars are picked up with variation in the square pattern of the latticework. The effect is to anchor the structure solidly to the paver patio.

Climbing vines filter out some of the afternoon sun and provide a pleasant welcoming contrast against the painted surfaces.

The predominant greens of the foliage background and the mood they create would be disturbed by an infusion of color. Yet, this scene needs just a touch of the colorful, which the container flowers provide nicely.

Wrought-iron furniture, though structurally solid, brings a kind of French-Quarter filagree to this scene, an unusual delicacy that balances the mass of the overhead. How effortlessly a few details create ambience and theme.

Contrasting textures and colors create comfortable harmony in this conversation space. The pergola provides some shade, but is designed more to act as an architectural element framing the rest of the design.

Comfortable furniture will make you want to stay by the fire. Commercial fireplaces, both gas-fired or built to burn logs, are made in such variety that they will fit any decor. If you're looking for a focal point to fill out your get-together space, you won't have to look any further. Exercise care when choosing fireplaces. They can easily dominate even moderately sized spaces. Here, the mass of the unit is balanced by the solid wall behind it.

A gathering spot for all seasons. If you live in a climate subject to inclement weather, include a screened deck in your plans. This design offers plenty of both visual and actual access to the open-air deck outside. The blending of spaces is so skillful, the roofed space seems like part of the outdoors.

A large deck or patio can accommodate many functions, but give each space its own identity.

Levels help define areas. A few steps up or down tells guests they're entering a new space. Each of the levels of this outdoor space, tied together with steps, has a specific purpose and eases the the transition from the house and enclosed gazebo to the pool and yard. Patios or decks which contain no distinction between spaces leave guests feeling lost. In that way, a deck or patio resembles the open country, and steps act like landmarks.

Grilling station is convenient to both pool and attached gazebo, but far enough from dining areas to keep smoke from annoying the dinner party.

Wide top rails double as mini-countertops for cooking and serving utensils.

Framed lattice screening hides the unattractive underside of the deck and helps anchor it visually to the landscape.

Mortared stone bench provides seating at the axis of sitting and pool spaces.

Short flights of stairs break the long vertical drop into more comfortable sections.

This deck can handle both large and small groups with ease and not just because of its size. The roofed bench is clearly defined as a place for small groups (or two folks in quiet conversation). So is the shaded table. The area between them is designed for larger parties and separates the two areas when different family members are engaged in different activities.

Light open-weave furniture continues the unifying theme of the lattice railing. Lattice lets the breezes in but provides some filtered privacy.

Roofed gazebo offers separate, well-defined space for large gatherings sheltered from the rain or harsh sun.

The simple lines of the overhead rafters provide a horizontal transition from the house to the gazebo, in addition to shading the large central deck area.

Hanging baskets and other container plantings inject colorful notes into the predominantly white background.

A defining style brought about by the painted surfaces has a practical dimension, also. Here it unifies the separation of spaces on this expansive outdoor deck.

Original terrain featured a small peninsula jutting out from the back yard. Removing it would have required grading expenses. Containing it helps define the perimeter of the patio and provides casual seating.

Circular pattern in the paving mirrors the curve of the wall and helps establish the identity of the dining space. Without it, the space might seem too open.

A raised flower bed and textured wall contain the terrain and help frame this outdoor kitchen. A large yard like this can handle a spacious deck or patio. Design your outdoor room ... scale appropriate to the size of your lot.

Expanding outdoor living space with scored concrete is an inexpensive way of enlarging deck space. Lush landscaping unifies the areas into a single entity for entertaining.

Open-wire railing infill maintains the panoramic view of the yard. Such horizontal infill may not allowed by building codes in your municipality, so be sure to check before drawing your plans.

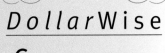
The lay of the land can affect the location of your deck or patio. Raised decks bring the perfect solution to sloped terrain. Here, the homeowners wanted a large deck for entertaining with access from their ground-level family room, but the slope of the land meant extensive grading. Instead, they opted for a raised deck with access from the interior dining room and kitchen. On the far side, the deck wraps around the house and provides a quiet spot outside the bedroom.

Portable propane grill is tucked out of the way when not in use and can be wheeled a few feet closer before firing it up.

Walkway provides access to the deck from the screened porch.

Detached, yet connected. This circular patio is a convenient get-away—accessible from both the porch and the kitchen, yet far enough away to be private.

Family Rooms

All decks and patios are recreational areas in one sense, and you can ensure that there's something for everyone by enlisting the ideas of all family members when you plan the space. Tables used for family or formal dining make great places for children's crafts—and they keep the mess that accompanies clay and papier mache structures outside, where they're easy to clean up. Decks especially offer a contained environment for toddlers to run free or engage the imaginary gears of their riding toys. Older children can romp in the yard or on the newest play structure, under the close supervision of parents relaxing on the patio.

Pools and hot tubs are becoming an almost regular addition to outdoor living rooms. So are firepits—on both decks and patios. Each of these features becomes the focal point for family fun and recreational gatherings. And with these features, the deck or patio becomes a natural extension of indoor areas—bringing the enjoyment of relaxed gatherings outdoors. Don't let the environment encroach on your enjoyment. Strong winds can cool an open deck or patio—even a heated swimming pool. The very trees that shade the spot might mean frequent cleaning. Add an overhead or umbrella to keep the sun out of your eyes.

Playful color adds fun to a family spot. When using such dramatic contrasts as these brightly finished chairs, make sure you've designed the space large enough to keep the intensity of the color from overpowering the area.

Curves are much more pleasing to the eye and mirror the natural lines of a landscape. The sinuous outline of this pool, combined with the waterfall, flagstone patio, and naturalistic landscaping, make it look like a natural feature of the site. Because nothing is exactly uniform in nature, freeform pools fit odd-shaped yards better than rectangular installations.

Locate chairs and other furnishings at different places on the perimeter of the pool to allow for different exits and to enhance the informality of the site.

Space for entertaining is reserved for shade, and the table and chairs add a subtle accent to the pool design scheme.

If you can see your deck or patio from the inside, you're more likely to use it. Patios and decks do best when they're visible from the interior, and sometimes only a glimpse will do. That way they offer a palpable invitation to go outside. Large windows, French or glass-paned doors enlarge the view of the space outside and make it inviting and easy to get to. Try to locate your outdoor room next to an interior room whose purpose similar. Put your morning respite outside a bedroom on one wing of a wraparound deck or patio. Party space works better when it's adjacent to a family room or kitchen.

Incorporating a sunken room into a deck or patio is a great way to accommodate a localized change in the terrain. Such an area would make a great place for outdoor toddlers' play, allowing space for a sandbox (without sending sand over the rest of the deck) and a clear view for supervision. Later, you could transform the space by setting in a firepit, hanging a swing, or recessing a circular table for sharing Japanese cuisine.

Above-ground pools are less expensive than in-ground installations, and they go up in days, not weeks. Their high profile makes a deck the ideal structure for seating and pool access. Such an installation puts the pool close to the house without cramping deck space and offers an easy solution for adding a pool in a small yard.

*Design*Wise

Jolly Roberts
Landscape Architect
Auburn, AL

- When planning a deck or patio, list the activities you want to enjoy. What furnishings will you need? For how many?

- What size? Spaces can seem smaller out doors than in. Draw furniture to scale on your plan. Leave ample room for moving around seating and tables.

- Sketch your yard on graph paper, noting good views, sun and shade, privacy, slopes, and drainage. Slopes will require decks, or grading and possibly retaining walls, to create a level space.

- The general rule is—keep outdoor activities near related rooms—dining and grilling near the kitchen, entertaining near the living room. Break the rule to enjoy great views, water, or other site features.

- A few dimensions:
  Dining for two—8' to 10' diameter; for four—12' diameter.
  Standing room—5 sq. ft. per person.
  Main passageway—4' wide.
  Wall seating—24" high maximum and a minimum of 2 linear feet per person.

CHAPTER 2

Style

tyle is that intangible quality that makes all elements of a deck or patio design come together in one unified composition. But just because you can't "touch" style doesn't mean you can get along without it. If the appearance of your deck or patio makes one pleasing statement, and if that statement expresses your personality in the landscape, you'll want to spend time there.

A number of stylistic categories have been lying around for years and they make this elusive idea of style easier to grasp. Broadly speaking, all styles fall into one of two sets—they're either formal or informal. That is, they're characterized either by straight lines, right angles, and symmetrical, balanced arrangements; or by curved lines, offset objects and a seeming casual approach to how things are laid out. These are rough definitions, of course, and there's a lot of latitude in each category. In fact, some of the most appealing deck and patio designs combine elements of the two.

Then there's the concept of theme. Using a thematic approach means you design your space so all the elements support a common "look." The list of themes is endless and ever growing. Look through garden and design publications and you're certain to run into Period themes (such as Victorian with brick-a-brac and lots of colors), Classic themes (think Greek or Roman with urns and columns), as well as Mediterranean, Tropical, Regional, Asian, Contemporary, Avant Garde, Rustic, Naturalistic, and Eclectic.

With all these choices, how do you decide? How do you find your style? Begin with this book. Note the patios and decks you especially like. Then expand by starting an idea file. Look through garden and design magazines. Clip out photos you like. Add notes about decks or patios in your neighborhood. Notice that the best-looking examples seem to "fit" the style of the house or the landscape. That's important. When you're ready to start your project, take a second look. Throw out anything that no longer appeals to you. Build your design on what's left. Don't worry too much about why you like one thing or another. What matters is that you do. Let your instincts be your guide.

Themes

If you're casting about for a theme for your deck or patio design, start with your house. It might just be a dead giveaway. For a turn-of-the-century, three-story Victorian, little details such as gingerbread gussets, scalloped trim, and paint that matches the colors of the house can make a deck a perfect extension of your home. A residential four-square or arts-and-crafts bungalow would be better served by flagstone or the rough texture of tumbled, earth-tone pavers. The horizontal lines of a 50's ranch could lead you to parallel decking on a ground-level platform or brick set in a running-bond. Don't force your theme on your landscape. Whenever possible, blend the lines of the design into it. Unifying a theme with its surroundings is easier and less expensive than trying to change what nature put there.

A textbook study in formal design. This pool-side deck meets the true test of a purely formal composition—draw an imaginary line down the center, and both sides are perfect mirror images of each other.

Straight lines in the paving, railing, pool, and borders are the hallmark of of formal styles.

Sculpted arbors, even-numbered planters, balanced arrangement, and tightly clipped hedges help frame and define the view of the pool.

The untreated cedar arbor will gently age to a classic grey, taking on a hue much like the dog-eared privacy fence behind the space.

Blooming vines and climbers help "decorate" the fence, adding color—but not too much—to its neutral background. The plants have been specifically chosen so their bloom color matches the general red tones sprinkled through the site.

The rough, but solid pine table is adorned with complementary blue and white ceramic tile.

Painted ice-cream-parlor chairs from a bygone era add reds, blues, yellows and greens to this colorful composition.

In an eclectic setting, almost anything goes, provided it feels right.

What looks like an almost random collection of objects and colors is really the result of careful planning. This kind of apparent simplicity does not happen by accident.

A regional design style will incorporate materials, textures, and plants that are at home in the local environment. Here, the colors and textures of the stone patio echo those of the stones the nearby hills. Desert plantings set against the adobe walls complete this Southwest theme.

Less means more in contemporary styles. Notice that each geometric unit of this design—the portico cover, the obelisk column, the windows, and the skirting on the roof line—displays subtle variations of shape and mass that make this design continually interesting. It shows how you can do amazing things with one basic shape.

Circular table, egg-shaped chair frames are forms "opposite" to their rectangular environment. Notice how the forward line of the chair frames imparts a sense of movement and creates a tension with the rest of the patio.

Oriental designs are easily integrated with almost any landscape. That's because their proportions are derived from nature. The basic rectangular units of this fence are arranged to impart a visual rhythm while providing filtered privacy. Just the hint of an arc in the roof line keeps the eye moving back and forth between the fence and covered pergola.

Insert of woven rushes adds contrasting color, line, and texture—just the right amount.

*Good design can bring the outdoors in
and the indoors out.*

A naturalistic design theme might seem to have grown out of its
environment. Such a design fits both large and small yards and generally relies on wood and
stone to make its impact. These two elements can be combined on patios, too. Flagstone paving with
river-rock borders and rustic wooden benches will nestle a patio comfortably in a wooded back yard.

Period styles should pick up after themselves. Most period-style homes get their definition from details—the particular use of lines, angles, and colors that makes them readily identifiable. These details function as the bedrock for adding a harmonious patio or deck. A little skillful use of colors and shapes—whites, grays, and rectangles—blends this deck with the overall architecture of the house. Even the height of the house, which is predominantly vertical, is mirrored in the pillars and balusters, offset by the contrasts of the sealed decking and horizontal expanse of the deck itself.

Color and pattern
can bring a taste of
the exotic to any
backyard landscape.
Some thematic styles, like this
dramatic Moroccan design,
revel in repeated colors and
patterns. Blues and tints of
red (here, pink) always complement one another, a play
of variety in the fireplace
design that is subtly picked up
in the tile paving.

A style doesn't have to
have a "name." By combin-
ing different elements, you can
achieve a cohesive plan that
belongs to you alone, not any
preordained category. Here, the
wicker benches and chairs—
Italianate or Colonial, depending
on your definition—add a comfort that seems right at home
with "tropical" plantings. Notice
how the scale of the foliage provides an environment in which
the furnishings seem to nest.

DollarWise

You can create a styl-
ish deck or patio with-
out spending a bun-
dle. Choose a regional
style with materials
and plants that are
local to your area.
Local materials reduce
shipping costs, local
plants require less
care, and regional
styles integrate them-
selves immediately
into the environment.

Landscaping

Aside from the basic elements that define the shape and configuration of a deck or patio, perhaps no other element contributes more to its appearance than landscaping. Landscaping can mean many things—changing the terrain by grading, outlining the shape of your outdoor space with planting beds, adding paths to link detached areas, suggesting "journey." It can also mean doing nothing at all, by incorporating your new space into an existing garden or decorating even the most simple deck or patio with a rush of color in container gardens.

Point of view. Good planning doesn't show the effort it might have taken to achieve its goals. All of the elements of this quiet place work together so effortlessly that the viewer can't tell what was there originally and what was added by the plans.

Built-in bench seats border conversation area for small groups or for taking in the natural beauty of the garden.

Steps lead down from the main deck to the wide walkway, offering an invitation to the garden.

Foliage with different textures adds interest to the array of plantings.

Taming a wild space.

This deck and walkway certainly is not ensconced in the jungle, though it looks like it could be. Although not a deliberate attempt to create a tropical environment, the eclectic choice and arrangement of plants and flowers make this spot a hard place to leave.

Hanging baskets add color overhead,

and you don't have to be as choosy about placement. That's because overhead locations don't have to compete with ground-level plants for attention. Plants native to your area will require less maintenance and upkeep, but drip irrigation systems are easy to install, making hanging gardens easier to own.

Colorful flowers and plants are just about the only thing a deck or patio can't get too much of.

The shape of the planting bed and shape of the deck or patio go hand in hand. Scale the height of the plants to the scale of your seating. Plants close to the seating area should not be higher than eye level. The view from a low bench like this one would be blocked if the plants were tall.

STYLE

Container gardens offer a host of advantages to any deck or patio. First of all, they're easy to grow and maintain, especially if you group those with similar nutritional and sun/shade requirements in the same pot. Second, they go anywhere you need to brighten up a spot. Use them as accents or to frame a view. Put tall varieties in a row for some strategic privacy (it's less expensive than a fence). And move them around when you tire of one arrangement and need another.

Even a single bonsai tree or clipped planting can lend an oriental accent to a midwest deck, and it won't require you to change your entire design scheme.

A sunken garden calls attention to the tree and gives it its own special design status.

Plan regional landscaping to reflect the environment in which the plants grow naturally. The landscaping in this southwestern patio and reflecting pool reflect the realities of desert growth. Plants in arid climates have to fight for nutrition and water, and thus different species are seldom found growing in clumps or colonies. They are naturally spaced at various distances from one another, as reflected in this plan.

Gentle curves follow the contour of the terrain at the edge of this pool and become the determining element for the rest of the pool design.

Plants are more than instruments of aesthetic intent. They can be as practical as lattice (and prettier) when it comes to solving problems such as hiding that bare space under the deck. Raised decks can leave gaping holes in a design. Plant in tiers—shrubs near the deck, mid-sized plants in the center, and smaller flowers or groundcover in the front row.

*Idea*Wise

Planters can go anywhere on a deck or patio, and wherever they go, they impart a little magic. Why buy commercial units when you can make them yourself? Make them from 1x boards. Cedar and redwood work well because they are naturally rot-resistant. Use the same wood as the decking or railings. Fasten the joints with corrosion-resistant screws or finishing nails and set the planters on your railing or patio, or at the edge of the opening for a tree or shrub.

Planting bed at the edge of the deck eases the transition to the patio surface and softens the hard corner of the decking.

Even the scalloped pergola resembles the shapes of leaves in this lushly designed patio landscape. Small details such as these help reinforce the style of an outdoor room, and their clever shapes add a slightly humorous touch to the scene. All of the hard edges of this site use plants to soften them.

Stepping stones lead from the patio across the pond into the wooded area.

Add sparkle with moving water. This waterfall emptying into a small pool is part of a recirculating system built into the patio. It offers a refreshing bit of background noise to mask the clamor of the neighborhood, and the pool augments the naturalistic tone of the flagstone surface.

Landscaping is all about plants—and other things, too, like the ironwork that suggests an entry to this pathway leading to a quiet retreat. Large potted urns act as the gate to this site, and though they're not meant to stop intruders, they do set the area off by itself and help define its edges.

When your design meets a natural obstacle, incorporate it into the plan.

Make mature trees a feature of your outdoor room. Building a deck around a tree lets you keep the tree and an important ornament. Bring the decking within a couple inches of the trunk and keep the joists back far enough that you can trim the decking as the tree grows.

Stonework abounds in this pool surround, both natural stone and its fashioned counterpart. Incorporating the boulders into the structure of the wall makes good design sense, and it costs less than removing what ultimately became an attractive accent.

A small pond surrounded by rocks and plants looks perfectly natural at the base of this landscaped deck. Modern pond liners make such an installation easy.

*Design*Wise

Timothy Jones,
Jones Brothers
Construction
Oakland, CA

There's no end to the "inventions" you can use to enhance your deck or patio.

- Treat the space between railing posts as a "canvas." Cap the posts with a 2 x 6 and fasten "panels" in the frame with 1 x 1 nailers. Use thin copper sheets (wash off its oil coat to let a patina form). Draw shapes on thin iron and have someone cut them with a cutting torch. If you like rustic, seal the iron with a clear sealer.

For enameled color, get it powder-coated. UV-resistant plastics and tempered glass—obscure, patterned, or clear—will also work. So will lattice, which will also support light-weight vines for a lush green look.

- Put plants in the middle of a ground-level deck. Before you lay the decking, build a pressure-treated planter and line it with self-stick roofing membrane. Set it on the ground between joists. Plant a new tree or small plantings. Run a drip line to the box before the decking goes down.

- Before you set a brick patio, lay out flag stone in an interesting pattern on top of the bricks and outline the flagstone. Cut the brick on the outlines and inset the flagstone as you are laying the brick.

CHAPTER 3

Pattern &
Rhythm

*A*ll good designs, including those for decks and patios, display certain patterns and rhythms. You can't hear them, of course, but you can see them. If you employ them effectively, they can enhance the appearance of your outdoor room, making it more useful and enjoyable. Decking sets the stage. Railings help establish the tone or mood of the design. And all kinds of accents can embellish your main theme.

You'll see a lot of decking that runs parallel to the longest wall of a house, and there's nothing at all wrong with that. In many plans, parallel decking might be the best style. But take a look at diagonal and geometric patterns, too. Chevrons (v-shaped), diamonds, parquets, and herringbones can really put visual sizzle into your design. Balusters are commonly 2 x 2s fastened to the rail and the outside joists. Imagine, instead, insetting them in panels between the posts. Add a wide cap rail. Use tubular metals, wires, or logs (in a rustic setting), and you're well on the road to creating a work of backyard art. Then look around for blank spots in the plan (do this after the deck is up or the patio is down). Those are "rests". Don't fill them all up; you'll need some empty spaces for variety. Into the rest go the things you love that make your deck or patio truly yours—the trinkets and art, antiques and artifacts, marbles and mobiles—anything you want to spice up your space. Besides, haven't you been looking for a place to put those seashells you stored away in the laundry-room closet?

Decking

Picking a decking pattern is both an aesthetic and a practical enterprise. If you need to visually separate the outdoor dining space for your family from the place for parties, a decking pattern is a ready tool. You can also change the perception of space with decking. "Shorten" a long deck and make it seem wider by setting the boards perpendicular to the long side. Trim the edges to make them look professional. Above all, stick to the rule of scale—the less the space, the simpler the style (That goes for patios, too). Small spaces jammed with a complex pattern will look busy. Be aware that unique decking patterns will require unique framing to support the surface decking. And these patterns can be slightly more expensive since there is more cutting waste.

Alternating the orientation of the decking increases the visual interest of the design and "signals" the beginning of each succeeding step

In small spaces, distraction and decking work hand in hand to make this space seem larger. Alternating diagonals on the deck create "width" that isn't really there, painting windowsills to match the furniture, and planting a large shrub at the opposite end—all catch your eye and help you forget this spot is only eight feet wide.

Three pairs of double doors provide plenty of access from the interior. Opening the doors for a large gathering makes the deck and family room one space.

Wide stairs with angled access opens the deck up and invites guests out to the lawn.

Decking for distinction—of one space from another, that is. These large modular and alternating deck sections imply that each space has a different use. One is for lounging, one is for the propane grill, and the others belong to guests. Such sectioning also breaks up the visual expanse of the deck.

Unifying lines. Chevron decking, here with the corners separated by a central plank, draws the eye out to the landscape beyond. The plank-top table and slatted chairs are perfect choices, picking up the pattern of the composite decking, unifying the furnishings with their space.

Steps gently reduce the transition of a slope. Curved risers with "spoked" decking makes the steps a focal point in their own right. Achieving such a curved edge is accomplished by cutting a series of parallel slots, or kerfs, into the underlying framing members, which allows the boards to be bent into a curve.

*Idea*Wise

Paint yourself a charming pattern. If the additional cost of framing required puts a fancy decking pattern beyond your reach, try painting a pattern. Use high quality alkyd deck paints and alternate their colors and shapes using stencils. The paint will wear off, of course, but the wood texture and color showing through will only add to the charm of your design. This idea works best when you want to create the look of a quaint cottage and with gray untreated woods.

Railings

A good railing should call attention to itself without being showy. Of course it's there for safety, to keep you from falling off, but after that, the sky's the limit when choosing what kinds of materials you can use or how you can combine them. Just make sure that all the elements appear as a harmonious feature of your landscape. Be sure your design complies with local building codes, especially when using horizontal infill in your railing.

Black-iron pipe, or cast aluminum infill can bring a light touch to a massive railing structure. Clamp the rails together and drill an evenly spaced set of holes—through the top rail but stop short of drilling completely through the bottom rail.

Copper piping makes a nice foil for any wood tone and is easy to install. It can impart a modern touch to contemporary designs, but goes well with most deck styles.

Steel cable is an unobtrusive material for tying railing posts together—visually, of course. It's available in a variety of thicknesses. Make sure to use cable heavy enough to be clearly visible when installed. Hang fiberglass netting on brass hooks when the kids are around, and remove it when entertaining guests who want to take in the view.

Custom welded steel railings can be ordered to fit the specific dimensions of your deck. Paint them to match the color scheme of your design.

Alternating the width of railing boards especially the careful use of narrow lumber, opens up unique design possibilities. If your design includes post caps, style them to match the design or paint them to complement other painted sections of the railing.

Decorative millwork can come out of your home center, a custom cabinetmaker, or your basement wood shop. All you need is the pattern of your own design and a jig saw. For just a little time and money, you can design a railing that sets itself far from the 2 x 2 crowd.

Look for every-day materials that will complement the style of your deck. Here, copper pipe fit into common flanges works quite naturally with the tones of red-wood railing and the copper-clad post caps.

Paint can provide a powerful complement to a deck design, especially if it picks up the colors of the house. Here, the green and reds on the railing echo the window trim and red brick, effectively unifying the deck with the home.

Overheads

If you're having trouble defining the style of your deck or patio, look up. The right kind of overhead structure can work wonders in making your outdoor room a work of art. Even if you don't need shade, there's no rule that says you can't put up a pergola or arbor to help you define the space distinctively—grand and eloquent or beautifully simple.

Treat a bleak block wall as a canvas of design possibilities. All of the elements in this corner hideaway contribute to a novel solution for improving the looks of concrete block. Such details can transform an eyesore into space that's restful and appealing.

Where one more trellis might have been too much, and the accompanying planter would have cramped the space, a hanging basket comes to the rescue.

The pergola not only provides shade, its massiveness becomes the focal point, relieving the wall of that responsibility.

Extending the line of the pergola roof doesn't add shade, but it does help tie the wall to the overhead structure.

Lattice frames become ornamental trellises for the vines in redwood planters.

PATTERN & RHYTHM

All overheads go up essentially one layer at a time, even though they may look more complicated than that when you're done. Because they are such a strong architectural feature, you'll want to pick up some companion line or angle from the house in your design. Overheads covering detached decks or patios allow you much more flexibility.

Lattice panels make dappled shade that drifts across your outdoor room as the sun moves, increasing your comfort and adding a free design element to boot. Lattice also lightens the bulky appearance of an overhead structure. Lattice panels are available in 4 x 8 and 8 x 8 sheets.

PATTERN & RHYTHM

Design your shade structure with one eye on **design** and the other on the sun as it travels overhead. Be sure to orient the rafters to block the sunlight during the parts of the day when you plan to use your outdoor space.

Use the vertical elements of an overhead to frame an accent. This arbor was built primarily to frame the entrance to the patio, but placing the bench in just the right spot increases its visual importance and calls attention to its plain, almost Shaker style.

Plain or fancy, design your overhead structure to fit your style. Nothing more was needed on this platform deck than some on-again-off again shade for the built-in bench. The painted pergola also helps set the deck off from the rest of the yard. Shade for the table comes in the form of the umbrella, altogether a less expensive solution that met the homeowner's needs and the constraints of their budget.

Small color contrasts can go a long way in making an already enticing design even more alluring. Here, the copper brackets and "acorn" nuts have a structural role—they tie the beams and posts of this arbor together—but they do it artfully. The copper bar-stock inserts on the side panels repeats the patina of the brackets and provides a unifying detail.

Accents

Accents are decorative. They add the final bit of personality to your deck or patio. Almost anything can be an accent—anything with an interesting color, shape, or texture will create a focal point and draw your eye. Often, it's simply how you use the object that determines its success in your design scheme. Small open spaces are perfect for pottery and old tool displays. Put your favorite collections on shelves, but low enough that you can see them when you're out lounging on your deck chairs.

This classic scene is embellished by a pair of large planted urns and a traditional spherical yard ornament—definitely in keeping with the "rules" for this theme. The small lanterns in the front, however, are slighly lighthearted and not-at-all-classical additions that work precisely because they gently break the rules.

Fine art sculptures make terrific accents. They can't help being a focal point on any deck or patio. If you have more than one, space them judiciously, keeping plenty of room between them. This one was such a favorite that it merited its own niche in the curbing along the deck.

There's more than meets the eye in this oriental accent. Split redwood planks with their coarse texture are a nice contrast to the chamfered top row of the privacy fence and the inset oriental dragon.

Be careful with color. It's the most powerful design tool. All the blues, yellows, and reds against the yellow wall make this area immediately festive. Note the espalier on the wall. Wire frames help train vines or plants to grow in colorful geometric patterns.

Design Wise

James P. Teske
Landscape Architect

Centerville
Landscaping
Centerville, OH

- The "right" choice and arrangement of accents creates a composition in color, texture, and shapes. As you walk through the space with your eyes, you are treated to discoveries—little details become more pleasing and harmonious as you investigate. A lost door is framed with musical instruments, a brick wall becomes a family room display of knick-knacks, a swimming pool is turned into a formal fountain.

- It is always fun to use found objects. The adventure is to get the "look" without paying for it. Trash picking, attic searching, flea markets, or just asking around can get you started. If you can't find something by networking, then you buy.

- Putting the pieces together is fun—trial and error are how you learn. Don't be afraid to move things around each week. You'll be surprised how it can alter the overall look of your deck or patio.

- Outdoor display items, such as wine racks and bakers stands, are available at most patio supply companies. Seal wicker baskets with polyurethane to keep them from deteriorating.

Mosaic tile brings color and motion to a paver patio. Such murals are commercially available (some by special order) or you can install the pattern yourself.

A collection of things is actually one accent with many parts. Here the baskets on the shelves stand out visually because of the framed print and rack of bottles on the wall. The individual musical instrument "reliefs" surrounding the entry door take on more importance as a collection than they would if displayed as individual pieces.

Styrofoam planter decked out in boxwood, floats in the pond with the changing breezes.

CHAPTER 4

Materials

Choosing materials is at least half the fun of building a deck or patio—maybe more. (The other half is when you stand back and admire your handiwork.) It's here that you can start seeing the possibilities for your outdoor space. Don't be surprised if you encounter new ideas, some you never dreamed of. So keep an open mind. Every material creates its own specific style and lends itself to some uses better than others.

Perhaps when you see one kind of flagstone you'll find its surface too rough to the eye or hazardous to the knees of youngsters. Then look at bluestone, slate, or ceramic tile. They're smoother. So are some limestones. Maybe you love the rich wood tones of redwood and cedar, but your affinity diminishes when you see the price tag. With the right stains and sealers, you can get less expensive pressure-treated wood to look pretty close.

That brings up the question of maintenance, usually the last question and often a forgotten one. Almost all materials used on deck and patios will need periodic upkeep. Some more than others. Nothing in nature lasts forever, but sometimes natural aging adds to the charm of a material. Aged untreated redwood, for example, can be very elegant. And the occasional tipped stone in your stepping stone patio can add to the charm in a cottage setting. But when aging becomes decay, it's too late. Keeping your outdoor living space in prime condition will certainly be listed on your future calendar of weekend activities, so make sure to choose materials with maintenance needs that coincide with the schedule of your lifestyle.

Decking

Time was that so many decks were constructed using green-tinged pressure-treated wood that you might have thought this material was the beginning and end of your choices. Not so any more. Even as redwood and cedar continue to be popular deck materials, the list is expanding with synthetic products and exotic hardwoods from far flung places in the world.

Pressure-treated wood, injected with preservatives which make it rot- and insect-resistant, is less expensive than redwood and cedar and is readily available. Chemical compounds containing arsenates have been banned for residential use. Newer preservatives such as alkaline copper quaternary (ACQ) are less hazardous. You can stain it to achieve a variety of wood tones. It will require more frequent upkeep than naturally resistant woods and is often used for deck framing—posts, beams, and joists.

The chemical tinge associated with pressure treated lumber will fade in time. When cutting or sanding pressure-treated wood, wear a long-sleeved shirt and a respirator—the dust can be toxic. Trim pressure treated wood in redwood or cedar if you need to match more costly materials on the upper deck.

Heartwood starts out a rich red color and ages to a silvery gray. It's tough enough to be left untreated.

Sapwood is usually lighter and sometimes creamy in color. Seal and stain it each year to keep it protected.

Redwood's straight grain, lush reds, and natural resistance to bugs and decay have made it a prime decking choice for years. That's also caused supplies to shrink and costs to rise. Only the heartwood (from the inner core of the tree) is extremely resistant. If not treated, the sapwood will begin to decay quickly. Annual retreatments are usually required.

Naturally-resistant cedar makes a great all-around wood for decks. It's less expensive than redwood, but still not cheap. Keep it sealed with products that contain a UV blocker, and it will retain its rich color forever.

Much cedar sold today contains sapwood, which is not resistant. Decking and rails contain many joints where water can collect—pockets for problems. Seal them well.

If you think screws or nails mar the appearance of your deck, you can employ an invisible fastening system.

Light reddish-brown in its freshly cut state, cedar imparts a more casual, less stately look than redwood. But it is widely available in almost any size up to foot-square posts, if you need them. Most often it's more cost-effective to support your deck with less expensive grades and hide it with cedar fascia.

All woods age to a gray if left untreated; some, like cypress, more beautifully than others.

Cypress—more accurately, bald cypress—grows in swampy regions of the South, which makes it right at home in seaside (or similarly humid) settings. It's surprisingly strong for its light weight, and works easily. Even in its native region, it's an expensive wood —more so if it has to be shipped elsewhere. Like redwood and cedar, it weathers to a gray tone with a lot of character.

*Dollar*Wise

Lumber is cut in even multiples of length. You'll waste less wood if you plan your deck accordingly. If your first design comes in at 13½ feet, make it 14. That way, even though you may have to trim each joist a little, (some are a little longer than stated), you won't be throwing a lot away with each cut.

Create stunning effects in your backyard with woods from far-away places.

Ipe was one of the first of the exotic imports. Its deep brown to red hues are unmatched by any other wood, as are its strength and durability. It has the same fire rating as concrete (but is, of course, quite a bit more expensive). Increasing popularity is making prices competitive with high-end redwood grades.

Sustainable Forests

Exotic woods are experiencing a rapid growth in today's home improvement market—more rapid, in some cases, than nature can grow them back. To find out whether the wood you are considering is harvested from sustainable sources, you can contact the following organizations:
Certified Forest Products Council—(www.certifiedwood.org)
SmartWood—(www.smartwood.org)

Ipe can create stunning effects, as shown by this railing section, but is harder and not as easy to work as other woods. Use carbide cutting tools and pre-drill fasteners.

Cambara is lightweight and easy to saw and sand. First imported n the east coast, it is making its way westward, an increasing popularity that will bring its price—already somewhat less expensive—down. It is extremely resistant to rot and decay, can be finished with hardwood stains, or left to weather to a rich gray. You'll have to predrill this species, and stainless steel fasteners are recommended.

You might find Meranti reminding you of Ipe, and there are a number of similarities, from its light red to dark-red-brown color and interlocked grain. It is slightly more available and a little less expensive than Ipe, but requires carbide tools for cutting and predrilling for driving fasteners. Meranti looks best when installed with hidden decking fasteners.

Synthetics make deck care a thing of the past.

Synthetic decking materials offer all the design possibilities of natural wood—built-in planters, alternate decking patterns, and stylish railings.

Composition decking, manufactured from recycled natural products and resins, offers one of many maintenance-free alternatives to wood. You can sand it, cut it, and drill it—and you can walk on it in your bare feet, because it doesn't splinter. Some manufacturers offer a full range of decking, balusters, railing components, and fascia. Synthetic decking is not strong enough, however, for joists, posts, and framing members.

PVC vinyl decking—made from the same material as plastic
pipe—commonly comes in kits precut to your specifications. Its durability is making it a
popular alternative to wood products. Like composites, it requires only regular cleaning.
PVC, however doesn't hold up well to severe freeze/thaw cycles because it expands and
contracts. Check with the manufacturer to make sure it's compatible with your climate.

Some composites
capture the
"wood look" by
either brushing the sur-
face or by molding
wood-grain patterns
into it.

Paving

No other material offers as many design choices as patio paving. Select from a large number of different materials; each one comes in a host of colors, textures, lines, and contrasts, and each has its own installation technique. Don't forget that the spaces between paving materials offer colors and textures of their own. It's a good idea to draw out the pattern of your paving and experiment with it. The only material that prohibits this is flagstone, but some patios need a material that lends itself to freedom of expression.

Mortared brick can pick up formal or informal tones, depending on its surroundings. Here, the usual formality of a herringbone pattern is "roughed up" a little by the broken edges of antique pavers. This composite style is one that falls between the cracks, a wonderful example of the versatility of brick.

Sand-set brick has a hard time looking anything but casual, even in a classical setting. The deep reds of these clay pavers set in a basket weave pattern impart a comfortable, seasoned tranquility to both passers-by and guests.

A running-bond pattern is perhaps the most common brick pattern because it is the easiest to lay. Even this simple pattern set on a sand base creates variety and interest when the material provides a varied palette of colors. For all its versatility, brick can be a haven for moss in damp, dark locations, and sometimes you may have to reset a sand-set brick or two.

Alternating patterns separated by dark bands creates a formal air in this mortared geometric layout, perfect for a courtyard. Low plantings soften the hard edges of any paving and blend your patio into the landscape

Mortared bluestone—with its color variations—creates a dramatic statement for this patio. Flagstone comes in countless varieties. When you are making a selection, consider how the color and texture of the stone will enhance your home and landscape. All "species" of flagstone are on the expensive side and setting them is heavy work.

Nature put the mortar here between these flagstone pavers. It's not mortar at all, of course, but grass. Set each flagstone in its own sanded recess and brush soil into the joints to create a perfectly natural setting. Seed the spaces with grass or a groundcover tough enough to take the wear of being walked on. An installation like this may look effortless but in fact can take a long time to get a pattern that looks natural, not planned.

Cut stone is any variety of natural stone that is cut into regular geometric—most often rectangular—shapes. The most pleasing installations vary the design and position of the rectangles in an ever-changing pattern. This material lends itself equally to sand-set and mortared installations, but is more costly than uncut flagstone.

In woodland settings, flagstone seems capable of designing its own layout. That is what you're aiming for—a path or patio that seems as if nature put it there, not you. (Done right, with a little patience, and no one will have to know).

Words to the Wise

You may hear the terms "dry set" and "mortared" (or "wet set") when you're out shopping for paving. What's the difference?

- **Dry-set** (or "sand-set") paving is brick, flagstone, or precast pavers that are set in a sand base. That sound easy enough; but there's more to it. Dry-set installations require a 6- to 8-inch gravel sub base for drainage. Landscape fabric usually goes over that (to keep the sand from migrating down through the rock), then a 2-inch sand bed. The paving is laid on this bed, and the joints are swept full with fine sand.

- **Mortared** paving is any material adhered to a concrete slab with cement-based or thinset mortar. This installation also requires a gravel subbase, then a 3 to-4 inch level concrete slab, a 1-inch mortar bed, then the paving itself. Joints are typically wider than in a sand-set site and are filled with mortar or grout.

Which is better?

Mortared patios are less likely to heave during winter. Dry-set surfaces are generally easier to install and repair. Pre-cast pavers should be sand-set only. Ceramic tile always means mortaring the material.

Precast concrete pavers may look a lot like brick, but they're made from pressure-formed concrete, not clay. That means they're cheaper, but not any less effective than brick when it comes to designing the floor of a stunning outdoor room. In fact, precast pavers come in a lot more shapes than brick so you can make geometric figures that really stand out. Pavers are made for sand-setting and may (though rarely) require a little weeding.

Notwithstanding its "rude" material, most concrete paver patios will end up looking formal. That's because their shape dictates their pattern and the pattern repeats itself throughout the site.

This constant bursting of paver circles is both festive and alluring. Such a dramatic pattern is easier to achiever than you might imagine. Pavers come molded for such intricate designs, so you don't have to cut many pieces.

Splash some color in your design.

Color rhythms appearing at random help break up the expanse of grey tones and spice up this paver patio. To make such installations easier, stack common colors at key spots on the excavation and grab them as you need to fill in a spot with color. Stand back every now and then with a critical eye. Pull up a few or add some. Nothing about pavers is permanent until you lock the joints with sand.

Not so long ago, "patio" meant "concrete slab," dull, boring, and unimaginative. Concrete has come a long way since then, and today you may not recognize it at all. Many patios that appear to be flagstone, brick, or cut stone patterns are actually stamped and colored concrete, at a huge savings over the real thing. Because it goes on as a liquid (semi-solid actually), it takes on the shape of its surroundings, casual curves or formal straight lines. Within those perimeters, you can have anything you want.

*Idea*Wise

Tired of looking at that old slab you inherited as a patio? Don't tear it up just yet. If it's in sound structural shape, you can cover it with tile or mortared brick or flagstone. If you were already considering mortaring any one of these materials, you would have to install a slab anyway.

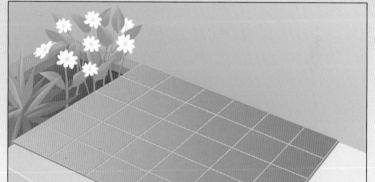

Poured concrete is a practical material for urban backyards that may not allow access by ready-mix trucks. Pour the slab from a portable mixer and color and stamp it with the design of your choice.

Stamping your patio is not your only option. Push small stones into the surface before it's set and wash away some of the concrete with a hose to create an attractive aggregate finish.

Stamped and colored concrete takes on the look of paving brick to outline the planter made from the real thing.

Saltillo tile, made from various shades of red clay and dried at low temperatures, lends a hand-hewn touch to any patio. It is a hallmark of Southwestern design themes, but is not suitable for patios in climates with freezing winter temperatures.

Ceramic tile is about as durable an outdoor surface as you can get. In addition, tile comes in an endless variety of shapes, sizes and colors. Choose an unglazed vitreous tile for a hard-wearing non-slip surface. Tile pavers, a foot square and larger, are available in stone look-alike surfaces, and cover a lot of ground in a short time. They're a little on the heavy side, of course, and like any tile, will prove more expensive than other pavings.

Combine materials when you need extra flexibility.

Combining materials can create a mosaic that makes a little extra space more attractive. Here the tile surface brings a nice design contrast to the redwood steps—a pleasing bit of additional space to the platform deck and an attractive transition to the surrounding yard. Notice how the earth-toned edge tiles extend the contour of the steps. Variations such as this create more interest than offered by a square or rectangular addition.

Soft materials, such as crushed granite, pea gravel, or wood chips go well with any material and offer a low-cost companion to hard materials when you need to expand your existing outdoor space. In most cases it will pay to keep loose materials enclosed in a border so they don't spill out on the lawn.

Hardy textures are surprisingly adaptive. They'll accommodate almost any mood. Here, rough-cut limestone set in paver-brick borders are a lot more effective as a contrast than either material would have been by itself.

This pool surround looks like a convention of regular forms. But the collection of cut stone, interspersed with red octagonal ceramic tile, creates a slip-proof surface with some effective visual cues that help define the sunning and resting area.

*Design*Wise

Christopher Mikol
A.P.L.D., C.L.P.
Certified Landscape
Designer, Professional

American Beauty
Landscaping, Inc.
Boardman, OH

• Try to be "true" to your home's era, character, and architecture. It can help reduce overwhelming material and design choices to a manageable two or three.

• Repeating the texture or color of a home's siding or brickwork in a deck or patio helps unite the two entities. Done properly, it creates both a visual and physical flow inward and outward.

•Homeowners who foresee a short stay in their current location may not want to make a large investment in their outdoor space—a stained or painted deck may suffice. For residents whose permanence is certain, pavers, brick, or flagstone might be a more appropriate material.

• Decks at ground level or slightly above can be a haven for mice, rabbits, chipmunks, and skunks. If you're thinking about a deck so close to the ground that you can't crawl under it, consider installing a ground-level patio instead.

• Combinations of different materials can provide a unique landscape solution. An upper deck can spill onto a flagstone patio at lawn level. A raised brick terrace can step down to a lower level with a contrasting material or pattern. Surround the lower level with a stone wall that doubles as a bench for seating.

Comfort

For all that's been said about the desirability of integrating a deck or patio with your home and landscape, there is one sense in which you want your outdoor space to be a world of its own—when it comes to the weather (rather, when the weather comes to it). Although you can't control the larger climate in your region, you'll want to make sure your deck or patio is shaded from strong sun, screened from harsh winds, and, to the extent possible, sheltered from the rain. In addition, you'll want it hidden from the view of neighbors.

Generally speaking, the north side of the house will be shaded all day. Where that's the case, you may want a detached site for your deck or patio, out of the shadow of your home. In many regions, south-facing locations will be hot all day, although they dry soon after a rain and warm quickly in the winter. East side sites are good for morning light and cool in the evening. Sites looking west will be cool in the morning, but can be unbearably hot by mid afternoon. These "rules" are only as useful as they apply to your site. If you live in the Southwest, your north-side patio may be the only cool spot you can find for miles. Out in the northern California bay area, a hot deck in the afternoon may bring welcome relief from constant cool temperatures. The key to all this is to individualize your site for comfort. Take stock of the sun and shade patterns in your yard. Get to know the direction of the prevailing winds, and in a rainy climate, plan for some way to get out of the rain. And no matter what region you live in, walk around the site you're thinking about and look for spots where you need a fence or privacy planting. After all, you want to spend time on your deck or patio, not on stage.

Shade

The primary guideline for creating a cool, shaded spot is "Use what nature put there and make shade where you need to." You'll want your outdoor room where trees, shrubs, even the walls and roofline of your house, shade it at the times of the day you'll use it. If your landscape doesn't offer built-in shading, add a pergola, arbor, climbing vines, or lattice to your plans. Even a single table umbrella can bring plenty of relief on a hot day. The best shade is filtered shade, a mixture of light and dark, not strong sunlight bordered by darkness. If you don't have it in the back yard, a side yard might be the perfect spot.

This shaded side yard has just enough room for a 7-foot platform deck. A minimum investment transformed a spot where grass wouldn't grow into a quiet retreat.

The benched-in corner was planned as the favorite space on this woodland deck, but the trees don't shade it continuously. Adding an umbrella creates two spaces, one for enjoying the sun and the other a shady spot to move to when things get too hot.

Strategically placed container plantings help bring some of the green of the wooded area onto the surface of the deck, unifying it with its surroundings.

The arbor gate will catch your eye, but the filtered shade from the pergola will keep you seated on this patio. Notice how the shade pattern casts a moving accent on the precast pavers.

Hanging baskets placed at both ends of the pergola provide a contrasting color and soften the hard edges of the rafters.

Access makes this deck a popular spot because it's easy to get to.
The redwood pergola keeps it comfortable. For much of the day, this pergola, with its high joists, shades the interior of the home (notice the shadows on the wall and window). When the sun gets higher, the 2 x 4 rafters and ceiling help shade the deck.

Clean, uncluttered lines and lattice panels create these twin pergolas. The structures not only shade this herringbone patio, they add comfortable, interesting seating spaces without overpowering the site.

Words to the Wise

 variety of terms apply to the various overhead structures you can build to shade your deck or patio. Here's a sample of a few of them, along with definitions.

Technically:

- An **arbor** is a freestanding structure with vines or climbing plants, sometimes incorporating latticework, which, depending on its size, provides shaded seating or signals the entrance to an area (or both).

- A **pergola** is an overhead, open-roofed structure supported by columns (or by virtue of being attached to the house on one side).

- A **lanai**—an Hawaiian word—is a porch, usually, but not necessarily, covered. Unlike a porch, a lanai will sometimes extend in a covered pathway beyond the building to which it's attached.

- A **veranda** is a porch, usually large and covered with a solid roof designed as part of the main structure.

For whatever technical differences exist in their meanings, "arbor" and "pergola" are often used interchangeably. What matters more than precision is that your audience (as in landscape architect) has the same definition you do.

How much sun gets filtered by an overhead structure depends on the size, spacing, orientation, and angle of the roof framing members. Wide rafters will, of course, make more shade. So will rafters spaced closely together. With an east-west orientation, the rafters will shade an outdoor space for most of the day. Set them on a north-south axis and you'll get east-west shade in the morning, sunlight beginning when "old sol" gets overhead. Rafters angled at 30 degrees will cast more shade than those set perpendicular to the framing. Then too, not all shade originates overhead. Fasten louvers or lattice to the sides of the overhead to block out the low-angled afternoon sun (makes a great habitat for vines, too).

Some sites are simply not made for pergolas or arbors. Perhaps what you need is an awning. Awnings are colorful, casual, fun, and less expensive. They'll keep you out of the rain, as well. They're also retractable so you can go from complete shelter to total sunshine with the turn of a handle (or flip of a switch). That's something you can't do with an arbor.

Now that you've put a deck or patio on your house, a gazebo will put a "house" on your deck or patio. Part screened porch, part outdoor room, part home away from home, gazebos are a remarkable invention. They allow you to add space with a solid roof to your deck or patio. That gives you a place to go when it rains or the weather is otherwise inclement. Depending on how you plan to use your space, you can enclose the structure (with the same material as your house, of course), adding heat for an all-season room, or leave it open, or screen it. And with any of these styles, a gazebo becomes a hot spot for a hot tub.

Lattice on the look-out.
Lattice panels are the choice of ceiling in this overhead, not just because they filter the sun. Here, lattice adds a design element— the dappled shade pattern that not only helps cool the space, but provides a constantly shifting play of light and shadow.

Privacy

If there were only one benchmark for the success of a deck or patio, it might be privacy. You might get by without shade, or quiet, or even comfortable furniture. But if you feel exposed on your deck or patio, you simply won't use it. That doesn't mean you should wall out the world. High, unending fences or walls will make you feel barricaded in. The best privacy is strategic: some structure or object between you and the unwanted viewpoint. Even with maximum "security," a view outward will reduce any consequent feeling of confinement.

Lattice makes a good privacy screen. It doesn't block the view (or the breeze) completely but screens your world just enough to dissuade outsiders from looking in. This site offers a good example of strategic screening. Notice that the lattice doesn't extend further than needed to screen the deck. Lattice is also neighbor-friendly. It looks attractive from both sides.

Grow privacy with vines and climbers.

Flower color is an important design element. Here, the purple variety of morning glories was chosen specifically to complement the blue-grey wood tones of the fence.

With vines like these morning glories, you won't get instant overnight privacy, but you won't have to wait too long. Morning glories really take off when the weather warms up, just about the time you start using your deck and having parties. You can choose blossoms like these that blend into the background or create a colorful display of reds, deep blues, and variegated pinks. Besides, plants don't know they're not supposed to grow on the neighbor's side, and they'll soften up the hard outlines of any fence.

Like this board-on-board design, fences with spaces are easier on the eye and reduce that fenced-in feeling. Other good board fence styles are boards-and-slats (alternating wide and thin boards) louvers (angled boards), and basket weave (thin boards woven between a center cross-member).

Strategic privacy sometimes means putting the screening at the edge of the yard. Nothing could be more open than this platform deck design. Yet it feels quite private, thanks to the cover of mature trees. The board-on-board fence along the lot line simply reinforces what's there. And although the Ipe benches are not privacy structures, they increase one's sense of enclosure.

Something overhead, sometimes just a suggestion, will help make a space feel more secure. Even a structure as open as these wire frames will do the trick. Space for intimate activities such as dining will feel more comfortable under a 10- to 12-foot "ceiling." Party space should have a cover up to 20 feet high.

Sometimes a solid wall—even the exterior wall of your home—becomes the perfect element for defining space. Doing so stylishly is an integral part of the design. Here, a decorative architectural element creates an interesting backdrop to a patio.

Windbreaks

Strong winds blowing across a deck or patio are just about as disturbing as relentless sunshine. What you want are gentle breezes, not gusts and gales. You might be able to find a spot on your property that's out of the prevailing winds, but if you can't, there are several ways you can tame them.

A slatted fence knocks the wind down to a gentle breeze. Any fence with an open pattern will make a better windbreak than a solid structure. That may seem odd, but research shows that a solid structure sends the wind over it and back down again at a distance equal to the height of the fence—just about where your dining area is. Open patterns diffuse the wind. You'll get protection up to 12 feet from the fence.

Patterns such as this redwood design are easier to cut than they look. The pattern is cut in several boards at once—to its longest length. Then the sections are cut to length in regularly decreasing increments.

Variable privacy, variable windscreen. The louvers in this treated pine fence are manually adjustable to provide some fine tuning of the breezes flowing across different parts of the deck.

Evergreens provide year-round screening. Whether it's privacy you want, or a windscreen, or both, evergreens will provide it year round. If you want to let the sun through to warm your house in the winter, you'll be better off with deciduous trees. Their leaves make shade in the summer and when they lose them, the winter sun can stream through to warm a cold corner inside your home.

The top of a fence line can be both decorative and functional. Adding the lattice panels to the top of this board fence extends the suggestion of an an arts-and-crafts design and helps reduce the winds. A solid fence causes the wind to vault over it and down into your dining area. Open patterns such as this filter the wind.

Tucked away in a tree-lined enclave, this cozy deck doesn't need any additional screening from the wind.

*Design*Wise

Greg Smith
A.I.A.—Architect

Adolph S. Rosekrans,
Inc., Architects
San Francisco, CA

• Walk your yard with a folding chair and inventory its natural features from different locations. Take your time. Watch how shadow patterns change, how the wind blows through. Where are the trees? When and where is the sun strongest? How long is an area sunny? Where are the best views? Who can see in?

• Take advantage of natural shade. Moving sunlight and wind in the trees will create constantly changing patterns and bring the space to life.

• Make "rooms" in your outdoor space. A trellis blocking a neighbor's view creates an intimate corner for solitude. An open area makes a good gathering place for friends and family.

• Privacy screens are really fences. Solid, high walls will make you feel confined. They encourage the curious.

• Frame a view with a wind or privacy screen. Panoramas are dramatic, but over time, a vista can become monotonous. An intimate garden view can provide hours of enjoyment. Bird and butterfly watching can make you feel more connected to nature.

Microclimates create their own weather zones.

Dark-color materials such as brick and tile will absorb heat during the day and release it at night. Use these materials to extend the use of your patio into the early evening hours in the fall. Light colors reflect heat and light and can brighten up a dull spot or help warm one that is cool.

A deck or patio at the bottom of a hill will feel cooler than one at the top. That's because cooler air flows down hill. Make sure you give the air an escape route as this deck does. Don't trap the air with a high wall or other structure, or your new outdoor space might be too cool for comfort.

Trees and plants filter the wind, and they make the air feel cooler. That's because they give off oxygen, and oxygenated air feels cooler. All of the elements of this site work to keep it cool—the trees and plants, the small umbrella, and the light gray color of the aged cedar.

Idea Wise

Runoff can make a mess of your deck or patio, as well as the surrounding yard and planting beds. Give the water a place to go. Line the perimeter with a drainage ditch and fill the excavation with gravel. For severe cases, lay in plastic perforated drainpipe and run the pipe to a catch basin or other place in your yard (not the neighbor's) where the water won't matter. Cover the pipe with gravel.

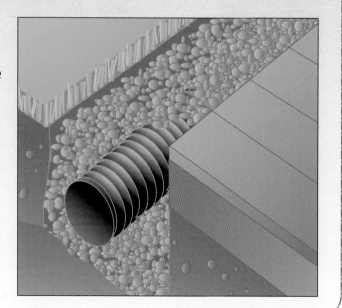

CHAPTER 6

Amenities

You've planned the major aspects of your deck or patio. You have a pretty specific notion of how you're going to integrate its style with the architecture of your home. And you can't wait to build it and test out all your visions for landscaping the space. Don't close the book on planning just yet. Why not bring all the comfort and convenience of the indoors to the beauty of the outdoors? That's what amenities such as outdoor kitchens, fireplaces, and lighting, can do. Such features increase your enjoyment of your deck or patio, and they let you extend the use of the space long into the evening hours.

Conveniences don't have to cost a bundle, but they do add to the "bottom line" of a deck or patio—the one on paper. If your first reaction is that you can't afford it, plan for the future. Outdoor kitchens may need plumbing and gas lines. So will a gas-fired fireplace. You (or the kids) might not be able to get along outdoors without the cordless phone or a small TV. That means an electric outlet and a phone jack close to a seating area.

You don't have to actually install any of these lines right now, but if you install the required underground utilities, and you'll be miles ahead when it comes to actually adding the amenities.

Outdoor Kitchens

A little extra space here, a few feet of decking there, perhaps moving the furniture closer to the patio edge, and you've made room for an outdoor kitchen, where the cooking is easy, the conversation flows, and your guests won't have to fan the smoke away while you're preparing the feast. Whatever you do, don't cramp your outdoor kitchen. What goes in it? Anything from a portable grill to a permanent built-in cooking center, complete with rotisserie, prep sink, and refrigerator. Counter space is important, but not crucial. So is some storage for utensils. With some judicious shopping, you'll find an installation that will fit comfortably into surprisingly small spaces.

Both the height and angle of the roof line keeps the kitchen shaded for most of the afternoon and evening.

Ceiling fixture lights up the cooking space at night.

Stone countertops add prep space and serving surface that matches the overall style of the patio.

Dining space keeps guests out of the heat and smoke of outdoor cooking.

Keeping the heat out of the kitchen.
When the homeowners discovered that their favorite spot for their built-in grill was also the prime target for the afternoon sun, they added this canopy to shade the space.

Bring comfort up-close on cool nights with a gas fired "mushroom" or "umbrella" heater. It's portable, and it will add a stylish accent while keeping you warm.

Using colors and materials taken from the landscape, this outdoor kitchen blends right into its surroundings.

Suited for family dining or large parties, one cook or several, this built-in stainless kitchen is a self-contained outdoor cooking island.

DollarWise

Don't have the room or the budget for a full-scale outdoor kitchen? Add a small patio platform to either a deck or patio, build a small storage unit for utensils close at hand, and add a tiled countertop that doubles as a prep or serving area.

Fireplaces and Firepits

Including firelight in the ambience of your deck or patio adds romance and charm, and it takes the chill out of cool evenings. Fireplaces and firepits are also practical. With or without outdoor lighting, they add nighttime hours to your space. Where you locate the unit depends on whether you want to treat it as an accent to the scene, a backdrop, or strictly as a warming place.

Most outdoor fireplaces are built as free-standing units, but can look right at home as part of a back wall structure. Fireplaces can overpower an outdoor space, but this one, reminiscent of a Southwest orno, or baking oven, avoids that pitfall because it's incorporated seamlessly into the wall.

Provide plenty of conversation space around your firepit at a warm but safe distance from the flames.

Flagstone "cross" designed into the patio helps unify the firepit with the paver surface.

Tile pipe lets rainwater drain out of the firepit.

Freestanding commercial fireplaces are available in styles that will fit any deck or patio design. Some models are equipped for open-fire cooking; others come with built-in oven inserts and timers.

Not all brick is suitable for firepits. Only firebrick will withstand the heat of an outdoor fire. Gas-fired units are a good choice for decks, and you can fire-up some models without leaving your chair—just push the remote button to turn on the electronic ignition.

Lighting

Lighting up your deck or patio allows you to use it at night and adds a large measure of safety to the site. A carefully thought-out lighting plan can give your space an enticing appearance that's remarkably different from its daytime personality. You can choose line-voltage systems, which require extending your house-current circuits to the outdoors, or low-voltage systems, which are easy to install and virtually shock-proof.

Hooded fixtures reflect light down to the deck surface.

Wide windowed doors let interior light flow out from the inside, reducing the costs of installing additional outdoor fixtures.

The right combination of both outdoor and indoor lighting helps create a warm glow across this redwood deck. The areas for gathering are lit just enough for intimate conversation, as is the deck surface that provides access indoors. The effect ties the interior space to the outdoors, without the intrusion of one space on the other.

Decorative lighting fixtures throw a diffused light on this paver patio, and their proportions match the blocks of the wall into which they're recessed. The main patio area is lit partially by the interior lighting and by hidden downlighting recessed above the windows.

Lighting fixtures can act as accents in their own right, as this arts-and-crafts outdoor lamp amply demonstrates. The fixture, with its copper roof, helps decorate the entrance to the deck both day and night.

Lights hidden behind white-glass panels in the "towers" on this railing transform the diagonal decking into a stunning nighttime boardwalk.

*Design*Wise

Jolly Roberts
Landscape Architect
Auburn, AL

Lighting your deck or patio involves the artful application of just a few techniques.

- General lighting is best for areas where activities take place. Down lights placed in trees and overhead structures provide a natural "moonlight" lighting. Washing a wall with soft light reflects ambient light onto close-by areas.

- Illuminate features beyond the activity area to avoid the sensation of being surrounded by a curtain of blackness.

- For drama, use accent lighting to silhouette, spot, or up-light garden features.

- To hide a light source at or below eye level, use fixtures with adjustable shrouds. Locate fixtures where they don't shine directly on a window, door, or path.

- Test lighting effects before installation. Lighting that seems barely adequate when competing with city streetlights may be much too bright in darker settings.

- For safety, illuminate steps, level changes, and paths.

This attractive lamp "shade," with its horizontal blocks offset between the back rails, makes a nice extension of the overriding style of the entire deck.

Path lights, either freestanding or mounted, cast light down along a walkway. Here, they add a decorative sparkle and provide safe passage to the nighttime conversation circle.

Commercial path lighting, the simple lines of the boardwalk and octagonal deck and the white stones of the gravel bed add an almost zen-like calm to this outdoor space.

AMENITIES   **121**

Pools and Hot Tubs

Pools and hot tubs can dramatically enhance the use of your outdoor space. They not only bring water to your landscape—a calming presence in itself—they also offer additional recreational opportunities for both family and friends. Both features come in a variety of styles, shapes and sizes—for above-ground and in-ground installations—so you won't have trouble finding one that fits the contours of your landscape. Make sure the location includes plenty of shade, as well as sunlit spaces.

Relaxing by the pool can be the perfect way to spend a sunny weekend day. Make furnishings and style as much a part of the experience as the water itself. Comfortable chairs, a table large enough for snacks or kids' crafts, and the pleasant touch of container-grown flowers help this shady spot complete the experience.

Whether below deck or above the surface, include space around your hot tub for beverages, snacks, towels, and just plain sitting with your feet in the water. Here, the pergola casts just the right amount of shade to cool the spot and helps define the space without walling it off. Bamboo wind chimes, some potted plants, and candles keep the ambience on the quiet side. The candle lanterns hanging from the beam, almost invisible during the day, come into their own at night.

Storage

Often last on the list and first to be forgotten, storage is something a deck or patio can't get enough of—unless you plan for it from the start. Make your first priority any yard tools and garden implements that don't already have a home. Add a garden shed to your plans, hang rakes and hoes from wall racks, or get them under the deck. If you don't, they'll end up competing for your outdoor living space.

Hide that gaping space under a deck with lattice or siding. Hang hinged storage doors with latches for access. This storage area has a corrugated tin runoff attached to the the joists above it, sloped so the rain runs off and keeps the mower dry.

A hinged bench makes the perfect place for storing chair cushions in the off season or for keeping baseball bats and the badminton net out of the way when they're not in use. You can also keep extra folding chairs off the deck and bring them out when the party gets too large. Storage benches such as this one will work well on patios, too. So will large covered baskets and plastic bins with cushions.

"Open" storage may seem like a contradiction in terms, but it's not. You may need a place to stash or organize those things which don't belong out of sight. Hanging shelves on the wall is one solution. Decorative accents like this old steamer trunk and wine cask offer you even more options. They provide display space, surfaces for open storage, and a place to put things that would distract from the overall appearance of the space.

*Idea*Wise

Decking can offer access to storage space below. Build a hatch door of the same material as your decking—about 3-feet square should be large enough without making it too heavy to remove. If the deck is high enough that you can stand up in the space below it, add a ladder for access. Store lightweight items such as rakes, hoes and shovels—things you can lift without too much effort. Or over-winter play equipment in covered tubs.

CHAPTER 7

Furnishings

They may not be the last thing you choose when planning your deck or patio, but furnishings put the finishing touches on an outdoor room. They have the last word on the style of the space. They decorate it, add to its comfort and can make a huge difference about how you feel about the space and how often you'll use it.

Since chairs and tables have that much "say" in the success of your deck or patio, they should obviously not be an afterthought. Choose them carefully. Certainly you want the style of the furniture to match the overall style of your design. So good looks, of course will rule. But consider other factors, too. Do you need to move the furniture around for different situations, customizing its arrangement for both small groups and parties? Then think "lightweight." Do you need lounges by the pool, something with a fabric that will stand up to the constant wetting and drying? Will the chairs spend most of their time in the sun? Then fade-resistant fabrics are a must. Durability matters, too. Buy the best you can afford. A little more spent now may save you twice the price if you have to replace your furniture in a few short years.

Fortunately, today's outdoor furnishings will meet every test you can think of. There's an incredible array of styles and materials—extruded, cast, and tubular aluminum are light and strong. Resin fibers, coated polyesters, acrylic blends, and powdered finishes make virtually indestructible and easy-to-clean fabrics and finishes that won't fade, chip, tear, or rust. You'll find everything from modern to English manor, from arm chairs to loveseats and gliders, dining and occasional tables. And, oh yes, don't forget the teacart—it's a great vehicle for moving snacks and dinners from the kitchen when there's not room for one outdoors.

Covered arbor lined with cedar posts leads the eye (and the guests after dinner) out for a meandering walk in the woodland garden.

Everything about this dining scene says settled and successful. The aged cedar decking, planting stands, and plank-top table create a warm invitation. Teak chairs offer a modern counterpoint to the uncomplicated lines of the table, which by the way, makes an easy weekend cut-and-assemble project. Pay special attention to your choice of table. It's the first thing people notice, and the right design will make them want to spend time around it.

Geraniums and spiky foliage soften the edges of this cedar bench. Small contrasting elements like these flowers can turn something as functional as a wooden seat into an accent in its own right.

Built-in benches work on patios, too. This laminated bench makes a striking addition to the mortared brick patio while providing comfortable seating in the corner. You can anchor almost any platform bench to a patio wall with sturdy brackets (and front legs, if you need additional support).

The perimeter of your deck or patio is an edge just waiting for a built-in bench.

Look to the architecture of the existing structure when designing your benches. Follow the lines of your deck. They'll almost always lead you in the right direction.

Dress up a built-in bench with planter stands. Building an all-in-one unit like this avoids the more complicated construction methods required for supporting a built-in bench on the joists—and the result is prettier.

Benches and planters go hand in hand. When you've built the back of a bench like this, you've already constructed one wall of the planter. You don't need much more than a "box" (stylish, of course) for potted plants.

Use period furnishings to finish an "old world" theme. Here, painted benches add a French provincial air to the welded iron fencing, a touch of Baton Rouge you can transplant to any region.

*Idea*Wise

If your deck or patio space is severely limited, built-in planters with wide borders can double as chairs and tables. Be sure to make them comfortable— the seats should be at least 18 inches wide and 18 inches above the surface of the deck or patio. Use the same technique when designing top rails. An 8-inch top rail will hold beverages and plates comfortably. In addition, built-in furnishings take up less space than freestanding units.

Kid-proof furnishings are a must for any outdoor space that has to double as a playroom. Paints and stray crayon marks wipe clean. Setting furniture right outside the entrance also makes a nice transition from indoor to outdoor spaces.

*Design*Wise

Chaden Halfhill
Silent Rivers
Design-Build
Urbandale, IA

• What's fun about designing an outdoor living space is interpreting the flavor of your environment. Decks and patios can be fluid and understated or expressive and distinct. Furnishings can do the same! They can blend into the space, becoming "one" with its architectural character. Make them an extension of your personality, a dynamic reflection of your lifestyle.

• When choosing furnishings—have fun! Color coordinate, or dazzle with pattern. Furniture can be objects d'art on the backdrop of decking or minimalist expressions that catch the essence of details found elsewhere on the deck. Find your voice and capture how you want to live outside. Funky or formal, it doesn't matter.

• Be inventive—use recycled logs for a bench. Find a metal craftsman to create a wrought iron table and matching chairs.

• Forget any "rules." Let yourself experiment. Try something you might not do inside your home. Outdoor space is very forgiving—it will welcome your expression.

Assemble an ensemble with colors and lines that fit your deck or patio. The red ceramic tile patio and roof tiles provide just the right background for the muted pink tones of this comfortable dining set, which comes complete with shade.

Furnishings should reflect all your priorities. This set of aluminum chairs and table are styled to suggest they're wood, and the removable seat pads add to their comfort. This site includes places for walking and benches for stopping and enjoying the view of the reflecting pond.

Simple, clean lines and high backs are the hallmark of modern comfort in outdoor styling. Many manufacturers offer collections of styles, with dozens of finishes and hundreds of fabrics. You'll find a variety of choices for any design theme.

Deep cushions are obviously designed for comfort, and the fabrics provide the ideal combination of fashion and durability, just the thing for a maintenance-free lifestyle.

Add convenience to your outdoor site with accessories.

This modern serving cart represents just one of a hundred styles of accessory items that can make using your outdoor space more convenient.

A side table brings small-scale convenience to any space. Tuck it into a corner on a small deck or patio, or set it off by itself on a large site to create a private getaway.

Resource Guide

A listing of resources for information, designs, and products found in IdeaWise Decks & Patios

Introduction

California Redwood Association
pages: 2, 3, 7, 11
405 Enfrente Dr., Suite 200
Novato, CA 94949
415-382-0662
www.calredwood.org
(p. 2) deck design by
Rex Higbee
(p. 3) deck design by
Gary Papers/Rick Kiefel

CertainTeed
page 8: deck
P.O. Box 860
Valley Forge, PA 19482
800-233-8990
www.certainteed.com

Iowa Outdoor Products
page 4: landscape and design
3200 86th St.
Urbandale, IA 50322
515-277-6242
www.iowaoutdoorproducts.com

Pine Hall Brick
page 7: patio
2701 Shore Fair Dr.
Winston-Salem, NC 27116
336-779-6116

Portland Cement Association
page 9: design
5420 Old Orchard Rd.
Skokie, IL 60077
847-966-6200
www.cement.org

Destinations

American Beauty Landscaping
page 31: design
5415 South Ave.
Youngstown, OH
330-788-1501
**The Ohio Nursery &
Landscape Association**
72 Dorchester Square
Westerville, OH 43081
800-825-5062
www.onla.org

**Arch Wood Protection Wolmanized®
Natural Select™ Wood**
page 12: deck
1955 Lake Park Dr., Suite 250
Smyrna, GA 30080
770-801-6600
www.wolmanizedwood.com

Archadeck
pages 27, 29: deck
2112 W. Laburnum Ave.,
Suite 100
Richmond, VA 23227
800-722-4668
www.archadeck.com

California Redwood Association
pages 14–16, 19–20, 24, 26, 29, 34:
405 Enfrente Dr., Suite 200
Novato, CA 94949
415-382-0662
www.calredwood.org
(p. 15) deck design by
Hooper, Olmsted & Hrovat
(p. 16) deck design by
Bonnie Brocker-Beaudry,
Milt Charno Associates
(p. 19) deck design by
Gary Papers/Rick Kiefel
(p. 20) deck design by
Richard Schwartz
(p. 24) deck design by
Dr. Robert F. Powers
(p. 26) deck design by
Douglas Fettling
(p. 29) deck design by
Rex Higbee
(p. 34) deck design by
Eli Sutton with HBM

Connelly Landscaping Co.
page 23: design
20145 Lake Rd.
Rock River, OH 44116
440-356-0505
**The Ohio Nursery &
Landscape Association**
72 Dorchester Square
Westerville, OH 43081
800-825-5062
www.onla.org

Crestwood Pools, Inc.
page 35: pool
220 Stage Rd.
Vestal, NY 13850
607-786-0010
www.crestwoodpools.com

DHM Group, Inc.
pages 27, 30: design
9 Professional Cir. Suite 101
Colts Neck, NJ 07722
732-866-0666

Iowa Outdoor Products
pages 28, 32: landscape & design
3200 86th St.
Urbandale, IA 50322
515-277-6242
www.iowaoutdoorproducts.com

**Oregon-Canadian Forest
Products, Inc.**
page 31: deck
31950 NW Commercial
P.O. Box 279
North Plains, OR 97133
503-647-5011
www.ocfp.com

Portland Cement Association
pages 30, 34: design
5420 Old Orchard Rd.
Skokie, IL 60077
847-966-6200
www.cement.org

Santa Rita Landscaping
page 18: design
1790 W. Sahuaro Dr.
Tucson, AZ 85745
520-623-0421
**Arizona Landscape
Contractors' Association**
6619 N. Scottsdale Rd.
Scottsdale, AZ 85250
480-296-2064
www.azlca.com

Telescope Casual Furniture, Inc.
pages 17, 21–22, 23, 25, 33:
table and chairs
85 Church St.
P.O. Box 299
Granville, NY 12832
518-642-1100
www.telescopecasual.com

Style

Archadeck
page 39: pergola
2112 W. Laburnum Ave.,
Suite 100
Richmond, VA 23227
800-722-4668
www.archadeck.com

AridScape Concepts, Inc.
pages 39, 48: design
7360 East Acoma, Suite 3
Scottsdale, AZ 85260
480-609-1221
**Arizona Landscape
Contractors' Association**
6619 N. Scottsdale Rd.
Scottsdale, AZ 85250
480-296-2064
www.azlca.com

Brown Jordan International
page 40: furniture
  9860 Gidley St.
  El Monte, CA 91731
  800-743-4252
  www.brownjordan.com

California Redwood Association
pages 40–42, 45, 47:
  redwood deck
  405 Enfrente Dr., Suite 200
  Novato, CA 94949
  415-382-0662
  www.calredwood.org
  deck design by
  Joseph Wood
  (p. 42) deck design by
  Bowie Gridley
  (p. 45) deck design by
  Richard Schwartz
  (p. 47) deck design by
  Timothy Jones

Centerville Landscaping, Inc.
page 43: design
  1082 W. Spring Valley Pike
  Dayton, OH 45458
  937-433-5395
  www.centervillelandscape.com

Connelly Landscaping Co.
page 46: design
  20145 Lake Rd.
  Rocky River, OH 44116
  440-356-0505
  The Ohio Nursery &
  Landscape Association
  72 Dorchester Square
  Westerville, OH 43081
  800-825-5062
  www.onla.org

Dan Druffel, Inc.
page 48: design
  8747 Morrow Cozaddale Rd.
  Morrow, OH 45152
  513-899-9111
  The Ohio Nursery &
  Landscape Association
  72 Dorchester Square
  Westerville, OH 43081
  800-825-5062
  www.onla.org

Designs By Sundown
page 52: design
  4501 S. Santa Fe Dr.
  Englewood, CO 80110
  303-789-4400

Iowa Outdoor Products
pages 44, 49: design
  3200 86th St.
  Urbandale, IA 50322
  515-277-6242
  www.iowaoutdoorproducts.com

Lakeside Lumber, Inc.
page 47: bench and deck
  17850 SW Boone's Ferry Rd.
  Lake Oswego, OR 97035
  503-635-3693
  www.lakesidelumber.com

My Garden
page 51: design
  301 W. Main St.
  Brookville, PA 15825
  814-849-1231
  Pennsylvania Landscape
  & Nursery Association
  5860 Saltsburg Rd.
  Pittsburgh, PA 15235
  412-793-1765

Plantique, Inc.
page 51: design
  6344 Schantz Rd.
  Allentown, PA 18104
  610-395-6940
  www.plantique.com

Portland Cement Association
pages 36, 50: design
  5420 Old Orchard Rd.
  Skokie, IL 60077
  847-966-6200
  www.cement.org

Telescope Casual Furniture, Inc.
pages 38, 43: table and chairs
  85 Church St.
  P.O. Box 299
  Granville, NY 12832
  518-642-1100
  www.telescopecasual.com

TimberTech
page 52: design
  894 Prairie Ave.
  Wilmington, OH 45177
  800-307-7780
  www.timbertech.com

Pattern & Rhythm

Archadeck
pages 57, 59, 66, 68: deck
  2112 W. Laburnum Ave.,
  Suite 100
  Richmond, VA 23227
  800-722-4668
  www.archadeck.com

Boyce Landscape Managment
page 71: design
  2249 E. Rose Garden Loop
  Phoenix, AZ 85250
  602-404-0219
  Arizona Landscape
  Contractors' Association
  6619 N. Scottsdale Rd.
  Scottsdale, AZ 85250
  480-296-2064
  www.azlca.com

California Redwood Association
pages 56, 57, 61, 62, 63, 64–65, 69:
  405 Enfrente Dr., Suite 200
  Novato, CA 94949
  415-382-0662
  www.calredwood.org
  deck design by
  Gary Cushenberry
  (p. 57) deck design by
  Decks Unlimited

(p. 61, bottom) deck
design by Gary Papers/
  Rick Kiefel
(p. 63, top) deck
design by Joseph D. Wood
(p. 63, bottom) deck design
by Ernie Rielly
(p. 64) deck design by
Gary Cushenberry
(p. 65) design by
Eli Sutton with HBM
(p. 69) design by
Landscape Architects, Inc.
(p. 69) fence design by
Marty Reutinger

Centerville Landscaping, Inc.
page 71: design
  1082 W. Spring Valley Pike
  Dayton, OH 45458
  937-433-5395
  www.centervillelandscape.com

Decking Northwest
page 62: deck
  5775 Willow Lane
  Lake Oswego, OR 97035
  503-697-9288
  www.deckingnw.com

Deckorators, Inc.
page 60: railing
  50 Crestwood Executive Center
  Crestwood, MO 63126
  800-332-5724
  www.deckorators.com

Elk Composite Building Products,
Inc. (CrossTimbers)
page 58: deck
  15500 West 108th St.
  Lenexa, KS 66219
  866-322-7452
  www.elkcorp.com

Metals USA
page 66: pergola
  www.metalsusa.com

The Ohio Nursery
& Landscape Association, Inc.
page 71:
  72 Dorchester Square
  Westerville, OH 43081
  800-825-5062
  www.onla.org

Oregon-Canadian Forest
Products, Inc.
page 60: design
  31950 NW Commercial
  P.O. Box 279
  North Plains, OR 97133
  503-647-5011
  www.ocfp.com

Silent Rivers Design/Build
page 63: design
  3100 86th St., Suite D
  Urbandale, IA 50322
  515-266-6702

Sonoran Gardens
page 70: design
4261 W. Jeremy Place, Lot 2
Tucson, AZ 85741
520-579-9411
**Arizona Landscape
Contractors' Association**
6619 N. Scottsdale Rd.
Scottsdale, AZ 85250
480-296-2064
www.azlca.com

Southern Pine Council
page 67: pergola
P.O. Box 641700
Kenner, LA 70064
504-443-4464
www.southernpine.com

Timothy Jones
page 67: pergola
Jones Brothers Construction
5769 Claremont Ave.
Oakland, CA 94618
510-652-3561
www.jonesbro.com

Materials

**Arch Wood Protection Wolmanized®
Natural Select™ Wood**
page 74: deck
1955 Lake Park Dr., Suite 250
Smyrna, GA 30080
770-801-6600
www.wolmanizedwood.com

Archadeck
pages 74, 78: deck
2112 W. Laburnum Ave.,
Suite 100
Richmond, VA 23227
800-722-4668
www.archadeck.com

Brown Jordan International
page 93: furniture
9860 Gidley St.
El Monte, CA 91731
800-743-4252
www.brownjordan.com

California Redwood Association
page 75: redwood bench, deck
405 Enfrente Dr., Suite 200
Novato, CA 94949
415-382-0662
www.calredwood.org
deck design by Scott Padgett

**Capitol Ornamental Concrete
Specialties**
pages 88, 89: patio
90 Main St.
P.O. Box 3249
South Amboy, NJ 08879
732-727-5460
www.capitolconcrete.com

Connelly Landscaping Co.
page 84: design by
20145 Lake Rd.
Rocky River, OH 44116
440-356-0505
**The Ohio Nursery &
Landscape Association**
72 Dorchester Square
Westerville, OH 43081
800-825-5062
www.onla.org

**Elk Composite Building Products,
Inc. (CrossTimbers)**
page 80: deck by
15500 W. 108th St.
Lenexa, KS 66219
866-322-7452
www.elkcorp.com

Iowa Outdoor Products
pages 72, 84, 89:
landscape and design
3200 86th St.
Urbandale, IA 50322
515-277-6242
www.iowaoutdoorproducts.com
design by David Rowe

**Joanne Kostecky Garden
Design, Inc.**
pages 86, 87:
610-530-8752

Kayu International
page 79: deck
1868 Knapps Alley, Suite 208
West Linn, OR 97068
503-557-7296
www.kayu.com

Kroy Building Products, Inc.
page 81: decking
1859 Evans Rd.
Cary, NC 27513
919-678-4840
www.kroybp.com

Lakeside Lumber, Inc.
page 76: deck
17850 SW Boone's Ferry Rd.
Lake Oswego, OR 97035
503-635-3693
www.lakesidelumber.com

MJ Design Associates
page 84: design
614-873-7333
**The Ohio Nursery &
Landscape Association**
72 Dorchester Square
Westerville, OH 43081
800-825-5062
www.onla.org

**Oregon-Canadian Forest
Products, Inc.**
pages 78, 79: deck
31950 NW Commercial
P.O. Box 279
North Plains, OR 97133
503-647-5011
www.ocfp.com

Plantique, Inc.
page 85: design
6344 Schantz Rd.
Allentown, PA 18104
610-395-6940
www.plantique.com
**Pennsylvania Landscape
& Nursery Association**
5860 Saltsbury Rd.
Pittsburgh, PA 15235
412-793-1765

Pine Hall Brick
page 83: patio
2701 Shore Fair Dr.
Winston-Salem, NC 27116
336-779-6116

Portland Cement Association
pages 86, 89: design
5420 Old Orchard Rd.
Skokie, IL 60077
847-966-6200
www.cement.org

River Valley Landscapes
page 92:
717-252-1894
www.rivervalleylandscapes.com

Telescope Casual Furniture, Inc.
pages 77, 82–83, 90, 92:
table and chairs
85 Church St.
P.O. Box 299
Granville, NY 12832
518-642-1100
www.telescopecasual.com

Timothy Jones
page 91: design
Jones Brothers Construction
5769 Claremont Ave.
Oakland, CA 94618
510-652-3561
www.jonesbro.com

W.D. Wells & Associates, Inc.
page 83: design
190 Woodcrest Rd.
West Grove, PA 19390
610-869-3883
www.wdwells.com
**Pennsylvania Landscape
& Nursery Association**
5860 Saltsbury Rd.
Pittsburgh, PA 15235
412-793-1765

**Western Red Cedar Lumber
Association**
page 76: deck
1220-555 Burrard St.
Vancouver, British Columbia,
Canada V7X1S7
604-684-0266
www.wrcla.org

Comfort

Archadeck
pages 101, 104, 109, 110–111:
deck and gazebo by
2112 W. Laburnum Ave.,
Suite 100
Richmond, VA 23227
800-722-4668
www.archadeck.com

California Redwood Association
pages 98, 101, 105–106:
redwood pergola, deck
405 Enfrente Dr., Suite 200
Novato, CA 94949
415-382-0662
www.calredwood.org
(p. 98) deck design by
Mark Becker
(p. 105) deck design by
Gary Papers/Rick Kiefel
(p. 106, both) fence design
by Vineyard Construction

CertainTeed
page 97: deck
P.O. Box 860
Valley Forge, PA 19482
800-233-8990
www.certainteed.com

Decking Northwest
page 108: deck
5775 Willow Lane
Lake Oswego, OR 97035
503-697-9288
www.deckingnw.com

Finlandscape, Inc.
page 98: design
740-927-1994
www.finlandscape.com
**The Ohio Nursery &
Landscape Association**
72 Dorchester Square
Westerville, OH 43081
800-825-5062
www.onla.org

Flexfence® Louver Hardware
pages 102, 107: fence
112 Basaltic Rd., Unit 4
Concord, Ontario
Canada L4K 1G6
www.flexfence.com

HomeCrest
page 110: table and chairs
888-346-4852
www.homecrest.com

Iowa Outdoor Products
pages 94, 105: landscape and
design
3200 86th St.
Des Moines, IA 50322
515-277-6242
www.iowaoutdoorproducts.com

Kroy Building Products, Inc.
page 96: chairs
1859 Evans Rd.
Cary, NC 27513
919-678-4840
www.kroybp.com

LockDry Flotation Systems, Inc.
page 104: design
2700 Alabama Hwy 69
South Cullman, AL 35057
www.lockdry.com

Portland Cement Association
page 100: design
5420 Old Orchard Rd.
Skokie, IL 60077
847-966-6200
www.cement.org

Silent Rivers Design/Build
pages 100, 103: design
3100 86th St., Suite D
Urbandale, IA 50322
515-266-6702

Timothy Jones
pages 99, 108: design
Jones Brothers Construction
5769 Claremont Ave.
Oakland, CA 94618
510-652-3561
www.jonesbro.com

Amenities

Archadeck
page 124: deck
2112 W. Laburnum Ave.,
Suite 100
Richmond, VA 23227
800-722-4668
www.archadeck.com

Architectural Landscape Design
page 117: design
513-271-4882
installation by
Evans Landscaping, Inc.
513-271-1119
**The Ohio Nursery &
Landscape Association**
72 Dorchester Square
Westerville, OH 43081
800-825-5062
www.onla.org

California Redwood Association
pages 117–118, 119–121: deck
405 Enfrente Dr., Suite 200
Novato, CA 94949
415-382-0662
www.calredwood.org
(p. 118) deck design by
Craig Townsend
(p. 119) deck design by
Scott Padgett
(p. 120) deck design by
Mark Allen
(p. 121) deck design by
Deck Appeal

DHM Group, Inc.
pages 115, 117: products
9 Professional Cir., Suite 101
Colts Neck, NJ 07722
732-866-0666

**Elk Composite Building
Products, Inc.**
page 123: deck
15500 West 108th St.
Lenexa, KS 66219
913-599-5300
www.composites.elkcorp.com

Kerr Lighting
page 119: lighting products
10 Soper Dr.
P.O. Box 446
Smith Falls, Ontario,
Canada K7A 4S5
613-283-9571
www.kerrlighting.com

River Valley Landscapes
page 114: design
717-252-1894
www.rivervalleylandscapes.com
**Pennsylvania Landscape
& Nursery Association**
5860 Saltsbury Rd.
Pittsburgh, PA 15235
412-793-1765

Sonoran Gardens
pages 115–116: design
4261 W. Jeremy Pl., Lot 2
Tucson, AZ 85741
520-579-9411
**Arizona Landscape
Contractors' Association**
6619 N. Scottsdale Rd.
Scottsdale, AZ 85250
480-296-2064
www.azlca.com

Sven Gunn Designs
page 116:
4300 E Placita Baja
Tucson, AZ 85718
520-577-1515

Telescope Casual Furniture, Inc.
pages 112,122: table and chairs
85 Church St.
P.O. Box 299
Granville, NY 12832
518-642-1100
www.telescopecasual.com

Timothy Jones
page 124: design
Jones Brothers Construction
5769 Claremont Ave.
Oakland, CA 94618
510-652-3561
www.jonesbro.com

Furnishings

**Arch Wood Protection Wolmanized®
Natural Select™ Wood**
page 132: deck
 1955 Lake Park Dr., Suite 250
 Smyrna, GA 30080
 770-801-6600
 www.wolmanizedwood.com

Archadeck
page 128: deck
 2112 W. Laburnum Ave.,
  Suite 100
 Richmond, VA 23227
 800-722-4668
 www.archadeck.com

Brown Jordan International
page 126: furniture
 9860 Gidley St.
 El Monte, CA 91731
 800-743-4252
 www.brownjordan.com

California Redwood Association
pages 130, 131:
 redwood bench, deck
 405 Enfrente Dr., Suite 200
 Novato, CA 94949
 415-382-0662
 www.calredwood.org
 (p. 131) deck design by
 Jamie Turrentine

Decking Northwest
page 130: bench and deck
 5775 Willow Lane
 Lake Oswego, OR 97035
 503-697-9288
 www.deckingnw.com

HomeCrest
pages 133, 134:
 table and chairs
 888-346-4852
 www.homecrest.com

Silent Rivers Design/Build
pages 129, 130: design
 3100 86th St., Suite D
 Urbandale, IA 50322
 515-266-6702

**Sunbrella® brand fabrics by Glen
Raven Custom Fabrics, LLC**
page 134: fabrics
 1831 N. Park Ave.
 Glen Raven, NC 27217
 www.sunbrella.com

Telescope Casual Furniture, Inc.
pages 133, 135:
 table and chairs
 85 Church St.
 P.O. Box 299
 Granville, NY 12832
 518-642-1100
 www.telescopecasual.com

Timothy Jones
page 129: design by
 Jones Brothers Construction
 5769 Claremont Ave.
 Oakland, CA 94618
 510-652-3561
 www.jonesbro.com

Photo Credits

Front cover: ©Getty Images
Back cover: (center & bottom left)
 Lexicon Consulting, Inc. Photo:
 James A. Stepp; (top left) Courtesy
 Wolmanized; (top right) Couresy
 Timothy Jones; (bottom right)
 Courtesy James Teske.
p. 2–3: Courtesy California Redwood
 Association. Photo: (p. 2) Ernest
 Braun, (p. 3) Stephen Cridland.
p. 4: Lexicon Consulting Inc. Photo:
 James A. Stepp.
p. 7: (top) Courtesy California
 Redwood Association; (bottom)
 Courtesy Pine Hall Brick.
p. 8: Courtesy CertainTeed.
p. 9: Portland Cement Association.
p. 11: Courtesy California Redwood
 Association.
p. 12: Courtesy Wolmanized.
p. 14–15: Courtesy California
 Redwood Association; Photo: (p. 15)
 Dennis Bettencourt
p. 16: (top) Photo Doug Hetherington;
 (bottom) Photos courtesy
 California Redwood Association.
 Photo: George Lyons
p. 17: Courtesy Telescope Casual
 Furniture, Inc.
p. 18: Courtesy Arizona Landscape
 Contractors' Association.
p. 19–20: Courtesy California
 Redwood Association. Photo:
 (p. 19) Stephen Cridland,
 (p. 20) Ernest Braun

p. 21–22: Courtesy Telescope Casual
 Furniture, Inc.
p. 23: (top) Courtesy Connelly
 Landscaping Co., Inc.; (bottom)
 Courtesy Telescope Casual
 Furniture, Inc.
p. 24: Courtesy California Redwood
 Association. Photo: Ernest Braun.
p. 25: Courtesy Telescope Casual
 Furniture, Inc.
p. 26: Courtesy California Redwood
 Association. Photo: Ernest Braun.
p. 27: (top) Courtesy DHM Group, Inc.
 on behalf of Hearth Patio &
 Barbecue Assn.; (bottom) Courtesy
 California Redwood Association.
p. 28: Lexicon Consulting, Inc. Photo
 James A. Stepp.
p. 29: (top) Courtesy California Red-
 wood Association. Photo: Ernest
 Braun; (bottom) Courtesy Archadeck.
p. 30: (top) Courtesy DHM Group, Inc.
 on behalf of Hearth Patio &
 Barbecue Assn.; (bottom) Portland
 Cement Association.
p. 31: (top) Courtesy Oregon-
 Canadian Forest Products, Inc.;
 (bottom) Courtesy American
 Beauty Landscaping.
p. 32: Lexicon Consulting, Inc. Photo:
 James A. Stepp.
p. 33: Courtesy Telescope Casual
 Furniture, Inc.

p. 34: (top) Portland Cement
 Association; (bottom) Courtesy
 California Redwood Association.
 Photo: Ernest Braun.
p. 35: Courtesy Crestwood Pools, Inc.
p. 36: Portland Cement Association.
p. 38: Courtesy Telescope Casual
 Furniture, Inc.
p. 39: (top) Courtesy Archadeck; (bot-
 tom) Courtesy Arizona Landscape
 Contractors' Association.
p. 40: (top) Courtesy Brown Jordan
 International; (bottom) Courtesy
 California Redwood Association.
 Photo: Marvin Sloben.
p. 41–42: Courtesy California Red-
 wood Association. Photo: (p. 41)
 Ernest Braun, (p. 42) Peter Krogh.
p. 43: (top) Courtesy Telescope
 Casual Furniture, Inc.; (bottom)
 Courtesy Centerville Landscape.
p. 44: Lexicon Consulting, Inc. Photo:
 James A. Stepp
p. 45: (both) Photos courtesy
 California Redwood Association.
 Photo: Ernest Braun.
p. 46: Courtesy Connelly Landscaping
 Co., Inc.
p. 47: (top) Courtesy Lakeside
 Lumber, Inc.; (inset) Doug
 Hetherington; (bottom) Courtesy
 California Redwood Association.
 Photo: Ernest Braun.

Index

CREATIVE PUBLISHING INTERNATIONAL

Complete Guide to Home Wiring
Complete Guide to Home Plumbing
Complete Guide to Easy Woodworking Projects
Complete Guide to Building Decks
Complete Guide to Home Carpentry
Complete Guide to Painting & Decorating
Complete Guide to Windows & Doors
Complete Guide to Creative Landscapes
Complete Guide to Home Storage
Complete Guide to Bathrooms
Complete Guide to Ceramic & Stone Tile
Complete Guide to Flooring
Complete Guide to Home Masonry
Complete Guide to Roofing & Siding
Complete Guide to Kitchens

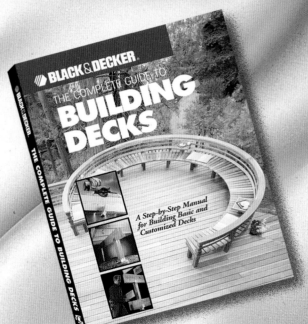

ISBN 0-86573-427-5

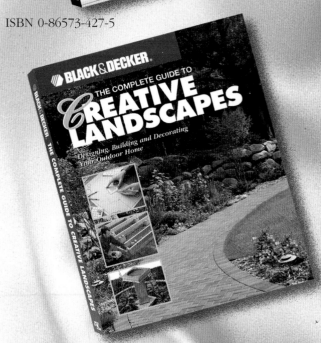

ISBN 0-86573-579-4

CREATIVE PUBLISHING INTERNATIONAL

18705 LAKE DRIVE EAST
CHANHASSEN, MN 55317

WWW.CREATIVEPUB.COM